PATRICK DICKSON

Florida Keys Travel Guide 2023

A Guide To Adventure And Relaxation

Contents

I

Part One

1

Welcome to the Florida Keys!

The Florida Keys is a stretch of islands located off the southern coast of Florida. Comprising over 1700 islands, the Florida Keys offers visitors the perfect getaway from the hustle and bustle of city life, with its beautiful beaches, crystal-clear waters, and laid-back atmosphere. Whether you are looking for adventure or relaxation, the Florida Keys has something for everyone.

This guide aims to provide you with a comprehensive overview of the Florida Keys, including everything from planning your trip to the top attractions and activities on each of the islands. From the northernmost island of Key Largo to the southernmost island of Key West, this guide will take you on a journey through some of the most beautiful and unique destinations in the world.

In the following pages, you will find detailed information on how to get to the Florida Keys, the best time to visit, where to stay, and how to get around. We will also cover the top attractions and outdoor activities on each of the islands, including the best beaches and parks, where to eat, and the nightlife and entertainment options available.

But the Florida Keys is not just about the islands themselves. This guide will also cover some of the top day trips and excursions from the Florida Keys, including Dry Tortugas National Park, Everglades National Park, Miami and South Florida, and other nearby islands and beaches.

Before we dive into the details, it's important to note that the Florida Keys is not just a destination, it's a lifestyle. The laid-back attitude and island culture is something that can't be replicated anywhere else in the world. From the locals who call the Florida Keys home to the visitors who return year after year, the Florida Keys has a way of capturing your heart and soul.

We hope this guide will inspire you to explore and experience all that the Florida Keys has to offer. Whether you're a first-time visitor or a seasoned traveler, we guarantee that the Florida Keys will leave an indelible mark on your heart and memories that will last a lifetime. So, sit back, relax, and let's take a journey through one of the most beautiful destinations in the world – the Florida Keys.

How to Use The Guide

This guide is designed to be a comprehensive resource for planning and experiencing a trip to the Florida Keys. To get the most out of this guide, here are some tips on how to use it effectively:

1.Start with the introduction: The introduction provides an overview of what the Florida Keys has to offer and what to expect from the guide.

2. Use the table of contents: The table of contents provides a clear and organized structure for the guide. Use it to find specific information on each chapter or section.

3. Plan your trip: Chapter 1 provides the history of The Florida Keys information on planning your trip, including when to go, how to get there, getting around, accommodations, and budgeting. Use this information to create an itinerary and make reservations.

4. Explore each island: Chapters 2-6 cover each of the major islands in the Florida Keys, including Key Largo, Islamorada, Marathon, Big Pine Key and the Lower Keys, and Key West. Each chapter provides an overview of the island, top attractions, outdoor activities, beaches and parks, where to eat, and nightlife and entertainment options. Use this information to plan your activities and make the most of your time on each island.

5. Consider day trips and excursions: Chapter 7 provides information on day trips and excursions from the Florida Keys, including Dry Tortugas National Park, Everglades National Park, Miami and South Florida, and other nearby islands and beaches. Use this information to plan additional activities or extend your trip.

6. Check practical information and tips: Chapter 8 covers practical information and tips, including safety and health,

money and currency, local customs and etiquette, packing list, and useful websites and apps. Use this information to prepare for your trip and ensure a smooth and enjoyable experience.

By using this guide, you will have all the information you need to plan and experience a trip to the Florida Keys. Whether you're looking for adventure, relaxation, or a little bit of both, the Florida Keys has something for everyone. So, grab your sunscreen, pack your bags, and get ready to explore one of the most beautiful destinations in the world.

History of Florida Keys

The Florida Keys are a string of islands stretching about 120 miles from Key Largo in the north to Key West in the south. This unique archipelago has a long and interesting history that is closely intertwined with the history of Florida and the United States as a whole. In this essay, we will take a closer look at the history of the Florida Keys, starting from its earliest inhabitants to the present day.

The earliest known inhabitants of the Florida Keys were the Calusa and Tequesta peoples. These Native American tribes lived on the islands for thousands of years before the arrival of European explorers in the 16th century. The Calusa were known for their skill in fishing and shell collecting, while the Tequesta were primarily hunter-gatherers. Both tribes were skilled navigators, using canoes to travel between the islands and the mainland.

In 1513, Spanish explorer Juan Ponce de León became the first European to set foot in the Florida Keys. He named the islands

Los Martires, meaning "The Martyrs," in reference to the numerous rocks and shoals that had damaged his ships. The Spanish continued to explore and map the area, but they did not establish a permanent settlement in the Keys until the 18th century.

In the late 1700s, the Spanish built a series of fortifications in the Keys to protect their shipping lanes from pirates and privateers. The most notable of these forts was Fort Zachary Taylor in Key West, which was built in the mid-1800s and played a key role in the Civil War.

In the early 1800s, the United States began to take an interest in the Florida Keys. In 1822, a naval base was established in Key West to combat piracy in the Caribbean. This base, known as the East Coast Naval Station, later became the headquarters of the U.S. Navy's Atlantic Fleet. Key West also became a major center for the cigar-making industry, with thousands of Cuban immigrants settling in the area in the late 1800s.

During the 20th century, the Florida Keys experienced significant growth and development. The construction of the Overseas Highway in the 1920s, which connected the islands to the mainland, made the area more accessible to tourists and residents alike. The Keys also became a popular destination for artists, writers, and other creative types, with luminaries such as Ernest Hemingway and Tennessee Williams making their homes in the area.

In the 1960s and 1970s, the Florida Keys were a center of activity for the counterculture movement. Hippies and other young people flocked to the area, drawn by its laid-back lifestyle and natural beauty. This era also saw the rise of the environmental movement, with activists working to protect the fragile ecosystems of the Keys from development and pollution.

Today, the Florida Keys remain a popular destination for tourists from all over the world. The area's unique blend of history, culture, and natural beauty continues to draw visitors who are looking for a one-of-a-kind vacation experience. The Keys are also home to a thriving marine industry, with fishing, diving, and other water sports being popular activities.

Despite its long and fascinating history, the Florida Keys face numerous challenges in the present day. Rising sea levels and other environmental factors threaten the delicate balance of the Keys' ecosystems, while development and tourism can put a strain on the area's resources. Nevertheless, the people of the Keys remain committed to preserving their unique way of life and protecting the natural beauty of their home.

II

Part Two

2

Planning Your Trip to the Florida Keys

C hapter 1 of this Florida Keys travel guide is all about
planning your trip. In this chapter, we will provide you
with essential information to help you plan your visit to
the Florida Keys, including when to go, how to get there, getting
around, accommodations, and budgeting.

Planning a trip can be overwhelming, especially when you are
visiting a new destination. We understand this, and that's why
we have included everything you need to know in this chapter
to make your trip planning as stress-free as possible.

In this chapter, we will discuss the best time to visit the Florida
Keys based on weather, events, and crowds. We will also provide
information on the various transportation options available to
get to the Florida Keys, including flights, rental cars, and shuttle
services.

Once you've arrived, we will guide you through the various
modes of transportation available to get around the islands,

including rental cars, taxis, and public transportation. We will also provide an overview of the various types of accommodations available, from luxury resorts to budget-friendly options.

Lastly, we will discuss budgeting for your trip, including the average costs of accommodations, transportation, food, and activities. We will provide tips on how to save money during your trip without sacrificing the quality of your experience.

By the end of this chapter, you will have a solid understanding of what to expect when planning your trip to the Florida Keys, and you will be equipped with the necessary information to make informed decisions that will help you get the most out of your visit.

When to Go

The Florida Keys are a beautiful and unique destination that attract visitors from all over the world. Located off the southern coast of Florida, the Keys are a chain of islands that stretch for over 100 miles, offering visitors a wide range of activities and experiences. When planning a trip to the Florida Keys, one of the most important factors to consider is when to go. In this guide, we'll discuss the best times of year to visit the Florida Keys.

Winter (December - February)

Winter is one of the best times to visit the Florida Keys, especially for those who live in colder climates. The weather is mild and pleasant, with temperatures ranging from the mid-60s to the mid-70s. The water is also relatively warm, making it a great time for swimming, snorkeling, and diving. Winter is also the busiest season in the Keys, so be prepared for crowds and higher prices.

Spring (March - May)

Spring is another great time to visit the Florida Keys. The weather is still mild, with temperatures in the mid-70s to mid-80s, and there is less humidity than in the summer months. Spring is also a great time to enjoy outdoor activities like kayaking, fishing, and hiking. Keep in mind that spring break can bring an influx of college students, so be prepared for crowds and noise.

Summer (June - August)

Summer is the peak season in the Florida Keys, with warm temperatures in the mid-80s to low-90s and high humidity. While it can be hot and sticky, the summer months are a great time to enjoy water activities like swimming, snorkeling, and boating. Keep in mind that hurricane season also runs from June to November, so it's important to monitor the weather forecast and be prepared for possible storms.

Fall (September - November)

Fall is a great time to visit the Florida Keys, with temperatures starting to cool down and fewer crowds. While the weather can be unpredictable during hurricane season, the fall months generally offer mild temperatures in the mid-70s to low-80s. Fall is also a great time for fishing, with many species migrating through the area.

Overall, the best time to visit the Florida Keys depends on your personal preferences and what you want to do while you're there. If you're looking for warm weather and plenty of outdoor activities, the summer months are a great time to visit. However, if you prefer milder weather and fewer crowds, the fall and winter months are ideal. Keep in mind that prices and availability can vary based on the time of year, so be sure to plan ahead and book accommodations and activities in advance.

In conclusion, the Florida Keys offer a wide range of experiences and activities throughout the year. Whether you're looking to soak up the sun on the beach or explore the unique ecosystem of the Keys, there is something for everyone. By considering the weather, crowds, and seasonal activities, you can plan the perfect trip to this beautiful destination.

How to Get There

Getting to the Florida Keys is an adventure in itself. Located off the southern coast of Florida, the Keys are a chain of islands that stretch for over 100 miles. While driving is the most popular way to get there, there are also other options available. In this guide, we'll discuss how to get to the Florida Keys.

1.Driving

Driving is by far the most popular way to get to the Florida Keys. The Overseas Highway, also known as US 1, connects the Keys to the mainland of Florida. The highway is a scenic drive that crosses over 42 bridges and takes you through the heart of the Florida Keys. The drive from Miami to Key West takes about three and a half hours, depending on traffic and weather conditions.

If you're driving from out of state, you can take I-95 south to Florida City, then take the Florida Turnpike south to US 1. From there, follow the signs to the Florida Keys. Keep in mind that there can be heavy traffic during peak travel times, so be prepared for delays.

2. Flying

Flying is another option for getting to the Florida Keys. The main airport in the area is Key West International Airport, which is located in the city of Key West. Several airlines offer direct flights to Key West from major cities in Florida and the eastern United States. If you're coming from out of state, you may need to connect through a larger airport like Miami or Fort Lauderdale.

Another option is to fly into Miami International Airport or Fort Lauderdale-Hollywood International Airport and rent a car to drive to the Keys. This can be a good option if you want to explore other parts of Florida before or after your visit to the Keys.

3. Boating

Boating is another popular way to get to the Florida Keys, especially for those who own their own boats or who are chartering a yacht. There are several marinas and harbors throughout the Keys where you can dock your boat. Some of the most popular boating destinations in the Keys include Marathon, Key West, and Islamorada.

If you don't have your own boat, there are several companies that offer boat rentals and charters. This can be a great way to explore the Keys at your own pace and see some of the more remote islands and coves. Keep in mind that boating can be dangerous, especially during hurricane season. Be sure to check weather conditions and safety regulations before embarking on a boating trip.

4. Public Transportation

While public transportation is not as popular in the Florida Keys as it is in other parts of Florida, there are still some options available. The Key West Transit bus system operates throughout Key West and the Lower Keys, with several routes that connect to popular tourist destinations like the Southernmost Point and the Ernest Hemingway Home and Museum.

There are also several shuttle services that operate between Miami and the Keys. These services offer door-to-door transportation and can be a good option if you don't want to rent a car or drive yourself. Keep in mind that public transportation can be slow and may not be as convenient as driving or flying.

Tips for Getting to the Florida Keys

No matter how you plan to get to the Florida Keys, there are a few things to keep in mind. Here are some tips that will help you plan your trip:

1.Plan ahead. Whether you're driving, flying, or boating, it's important to plan your trip in advance. Make sure you have all the necessary documents and reservations, and be prepared for possible delays or cancellations.

2. Pack for the weather. The Florida Keys have a warm and humid climate year-round. Be sure to pack lightweight clothing, sunscreen, and a hat to protect yourself from the sun. It's also a

good idea to bring a rain jacket or umbrella in case of afternoon showers.

3. Be prepared for toll

One thing to keep in mind when driving to the Florida Keys is that there are several tolls along the way. The tolls help maintain the Overseas Highway and fund local projects and initiatives. The tolls can add up quickly, so be sure to bring cash or a credit card to pay the tolls.

Another tip for driving to the Florida Keys is to be prepared for heavy traffic, especially during peak travel times. The roads can get congested, especially in and around the major cities like Miami and Key West. If you're driving during peak travel times, be sure to leave plenty of extra time for your trip and be patient.

If you're flying to the Florida Keys, be sure to book your flights in advance to get the best deals. Key West International Airport is a small airport, so flights can be more expensive than larger airports like Miami or Fort Lauderdale. If you're flying into one of the larger airports, be sure to factor in extra time for the drive to the Keys.

Boating to the Florida Keys can be a fun and adventurous way to travel, but it's important to be prepared. Check the weather and safety regulations before embarking on a boating trip, and be sure to have all the necessary equipment and supplies. If you're renting a boat, be sure to read the rental agreement carefully and ask any questions you may have.

No matter how you plan to get to the Florida Keys, be sure to take the time to enjoy the journey. The drive from Miami to Key West is a scenic and beautiful trip, with plenty of opportunities to stop and take in the views. If you're flying, be sure to look out the window and enjoy the views of the islands from above. And if you're boating, take the time to explore the remote islands and coves that are only accessible by water.

Conclusion

Getting to the Florida Keys can be an adventure in itself, with several options available including driving, flying, boating, and public transportation. Each method has its own advantages and disadvantages, so be sure to choose the option that works best for you. No matter how you plan to get to the Keys, be sure to plan ahead, pack for the weather, and be prepared for tolls and traffic. And most importantly, take the time to enjoy the journey and all that the Florida Keys have to offer.

Getting Around

Once you've arrived in the Florida Keys, getting around can be easy and convenient with several transportation options available. The most popular modes of transportation include renting a car, taking a shuttle or taxi, riding a bike, or even walking.

Renting a car is the most convenient way to get around the Florida Keys, especially if you plan to do a lot of sightseeing or exploring. Rental car agencies are available at all major airports, and there are also several agencies located throughout the Keys. Be sure to reserve your car in advance, especially during peak travel times, as rental cars can be in high demand.

Driving around the Florida Keys is relatively easy, with one main road, the Overseas Highway, running through all of the Keys. However, be prepared for heavy traffic during peak travel times, especially in and around the major cities like Key West. It's also important to note that parking can be limited and expensive, especially in popular tourist areas.

If you prefer not to rent a car, there are several shuttle and taxi services available throughout the Keys. These services can be more expensive than renting a car, but they can be convenient if you only need transportation for short distances or if you plan to do a lot of drinking while on vacation. Most hotels and resorts offer shuttle services to and from the airport, as well as shuttle services to nearby attractions.

Biking is another popular way to get around the Florida Keys, especially in and around the major cities. Key West, in particular, is a very bike-friendly city, with several bike rental shops located throughout the city. Biking is a great way to see the sights and get some exercise while on vacation, but be sure to wear sunscreen and bring plenty of water, especially during the hot summer months.

For those who prefer a slower pace, walking is a great way to explore the Florida Keys. Many of the major cities, such as Key West and Marathon, are pedestrian-friendly, with several attractions located within walking distance of each other. Walking can also be a great way to take in the scenery and get a feel for the local culture.

Public transportation is also available in the Florida Keys, although it can be limited and infrequent. The Key West

Transit system operates several routes throughout the city, with fares starting at $2 per ride. The Marathon Shuttle provides transportation between popular attractions in Marathon, with fares starting at $2 per ride. However, if you plan to explore multiple areas of the Keys, public transportation may not be the most convenient option.

Water taxis and ferries are also available in the Florida Keys, especially for those who plan to visit the smaller, more remote islands. Several companies offer water taxi and ferry services to areas like Dry Tortugas National Park, which can only be accessed by boat. These services can be more expensive than other modes of transportation, but they can be a great way to see the more isolated parts of the Keys.

In summary, getting around the Florida Keys can be easy and convenient with several transportation options available. Renting a car is the most popular way to get around, but shuttle and taxi services, biking, walking, public transportation, and water taxis are also available. Be sure to choose the mode of transportation that works best for your needs and budget, and plan ahead to avoid any transportation-related headaches during your vacation.

Accommodations

The Florida Keys offer a wide variety of accommodations, from budget-friendly motels to luxury resorts and everything in between. Whether you're looking for a romantic getaway or a family vacation, there's an accommodation option to fit your needs and budget.

One of the most popular accommodation options in the Florida Keys is vacation rentals. Vacation rentals range from small cottages and apartments to large beachfront homes and can be found throughout the Keys. These rentals offer the privacy and comfort of a home away from home and are great for families or groups traveling together. Vacation rentals can be found on popular vacation rental websites or through local property management companies.

Hotels and resorts are also plentiful in the Florida Keys, with options ranging from budget-friendly motels to luxurious beachfront resorts. Most hotels and resorts are located in the major cities like Key West and Marathon, but there are also several options on the smaller islands. Some of the most popular hotel and resort chains in the Keys include Hilton, Marriott, and Hyatt.

For those who prefer a more unique and rustic experience, camping is also an option in the Florida Keys. There are several public and private campgrounds throughout the Keys, ranging from primitive campsites to fully-equipped RV parks. Some popular campgrounds include Bahia Honda State Park, Curry Hammock State Park, and Long Key State Park.

Bed and breakfasts are another popular option for those looking for a more personal and intimate experience. Bed and breakfasts can be found throughout the Keys, with many located in historic homes and buildings. These accommodations offer a cozy and romantic atmosphere and often include amenities like complimentary breakfast and evening wine and cheese receptions.

If you're looking for a more luxurious and upscale experience, the Florida Keys also offer several high-end resorts and villas. These accommodations offer amenities like private beaches, infinity pools, and high-end dining options. Some popular luxury resorts include Little Palm Island Resort & Spa and Cheeca Lodge & Spa.

Another unique accommodation option in the Florida Keys is houseboats. Houseboats can be rented for a few days or a few weeks and offer a unique and unforgettable experience. Many houseboats are fully-equipped with kitchens, bathrooms, and living areas and can be used for fishing, diving, or simply relaxing on the water.

Regardless of your budget or travel style, there is an accommodation option in the Florida Keys to suit your needs. However, it's important to note that accommodations in the Florida Keys can be expensive, especially during peak travel times. It's important to book your accommodations in advance, especially if you plan to travel during peak season.

When choosing an accommodation in the Florida Keys, it's also important to consider location. If you're looking for a more laid-back and relaxed vacation, consider staying on one of the smaller islands. However, if you're looking for a more lively and vibrant atmosphere, staying in Key West or Marathon may be a better option.

Finally, it's important to consider the amenities and services offered by the accommodation. If you plan to spend most of your time exploring the area, a basic motel or vacation rental may be sufficient. However, if you're looking for a more luxurious and relaxing experience, a resort or villa with amenities like a spa or private beach may be a better option.

In conclusion, the Florida Keys offer a wide variety of accommodations to suit every budget and travel style. Whether you prefer vacation rentals, hotels and resorts, camping, bed and breakfasts, luxury villas, or houseboats, there is an option to fit your needs. When choosing an accommodation, consider location, amenities, and budget to ensure you have the best possible vacation experience.

Budgeting for Your Trip

The Florida Keys are a popular vacation destination that offers a variety of attractions, including beautiful beaches, coral reefs, and diverse marine life. However, planning a trip to the Florida Keys can be expensive, especially if you're not careful with your spending. In this chapter, we'll discuss some tips on how to budget for your trip to the Florida Keys.

· Choose Your Travel Dates Wisely

Choosing your travel dates wisely is one of the most effective ways to save money on your trip to the Florida Keys. Generally, the high season for tourism in the Keys is from December to April when the weather is cooler and drier. However, prices during this time tend to be higher, and the crowds can be overwhelming. If you're on a tight budget, consider visiting during the shoulder season, which runs from May to November. The weather may be a bit hotter and more humid, but the prices are usually lower, and the crowds are smaller.

· Research and Compare Accommodations

Accommodations can be one of the most significant expenses on a trip to the Florida Keys. However, by doing some research and comparison shopping, you can find some great deals. There are many different types of accommodations in the Keys, ranging from luxurious resorts to budget-friendly motels. Consider your priorities and preferences when choosing your accommodation, and be sure to read reviews from other travelers to help you make an informed decision. You can also consider alternative lodging options such as vacation rentals or camping to save money.

· Plan Your Transportation

Transportation is another significant expense when traveling to the Florida Keys. If you're driving from the mainland, consider carpooling or renting a fuel-efficient vehicle to save money on gas. If you're flying, look for deals on flights and consider flying into a nearby airport, such as Miami or Fort Lauderdale, and renting a car to drive to the Keys. Once in the Keys, consider using public transportation or renting bicycles to get around instead of renting a car.

· Budget for Food and Drinks

Food and drinks can also add up quickly on a trip to the Florida Keys. To save money, consider eating at local restaurants or food trucks instead of expensive tourist spots. You can also save money by packing snacks and drinks for the day, and opting for a hotel or vacation rental with a kitchen to cook some meals yourself.

· Plan Your Activities

The Florida Keys offer a wide range of activities, from snorkeling and scuba diving to fishing and kayaking. However, these activities can also be expensive. Plan your activities ahead of time and look for deals and discounts. Many tour operators offer discounts for booking multiple activities or for booking in advance. You can also look for free or low-cost activities, such as hiking, visiting local museums or galleries, or exploring the beaches.

· Set a Realistic Budget and Stick to It

Setting a realistic budget is one of the most important things you can do when planning your trip to the Florida Keys. Consider all of the expenses you'll encounter, including transportation, accommodation, food, and activities, and set a budget that you can realistically afford. Be sure to track your spending during your trip and adjust your budget accordingly to avoid overspending.

In conclusion, the Florida Keys offer a wealth of activities and attractions, but they can also be expensive. By planning your trip carefully, doing your research, and setting a realistic budget, you can enjoy all that the Keys have to offer without breaking the bank.

3

Chapter 3

III

Part Three

4

Key Largo

Overview of Key Largo

Key Largo is the northernmost island in the Florida Keys archipelago, located about an hour's drive south of Miami. It's the largest of the Keys, stretching for about 33 miles, and it's a popular destination for tourists who come to enjoy its beautiful beaches, clear waters, and stunning sunsets.

One of the main attractions of Key Largo is the John Pennekamp Coral Reef State Park, which is located off the coast of the island. This park is known for its diverse marine life and coral reefs, and it's a popular spot for snorkeling, diving, and other water activities. Visitors can take a glass-bottom boat tour to see the colorful marine life up close, or they can rent a kayak or paddleboard and explore the mangrove forests and shallow waters of the park.

Another popular attraction in Key Largo is the Florida Keys National Marine Sanctuary, which is home to one of the largest coral reef ecosystems in the world. This sanctuary protects the coral reefs and the marine life that depend on them, and it's a popular spot for diving, snorkeling, and fishing.

For those who prefer to stay on land, Key Largo offers plenty of other activities as well. The island is home to several nature reserves and parks, including the Dagny Johnson Key Largo Hammock Botanical State Park, which features hiking trails through a protected forest habitat. Visitors can also enjoy birdwatching, cycling, and other outdoor activities on the island.

Key Largo also has a rich history and culture. The island was once home to the Calusa Native American tribe, and later served as a base for pirates and smugglers. In the 20th century, Key Largo became a popular destination for artists and writers, and it was the setting for the classic movie "Key Largo" starring Humphrey Bogart and Lauren Bacall. Today, visitors can explore the island's history at the History of Diving Museum, which showcases the evolution of diving equipment and techniques.

In terms of accommodations, Key Largo offers a range of options for visitors. There are several resorts and hotels on the island, as well as vacation rentals, campgrounds, and RV parks. There are also plenty of restaurants and bars serving fresh seafood and tropical drinks, as well as shops and galleries selling local art and crafts.

Overall, Key Largo is a beautiful and diverse destination that offers something for everyone. Whether you're looking for an active outdoor adventure or a relaxing beach vacation, this island has it all. With its stunning natural beauty, rich history and culture, and vibrant local community, Key Largo is a must-see destination in the Florida Keys.

Top Attractions

Key Largo is a paradise for nature lovers, outdoor enthusiasts, and adventure seekers. This beautiful island is located at the northern end of the Florida Keys and is known for its stunning natural beauty, crystal clear waters, and diverse marine life. In this section, we will discuss the top attractions of Key Largo that every visitor should explore.

1.John Pennekamp Coral Reef State Park:

John Pennekamp Coral Reef State Park is the crown jewel of Key Largo's natural attractions. This 70-square mile park is the first undersea park in the United States and is home to some of the most beautiful coral reefs in the world. Visitors can explore the park's underwater world by snorkeling, diving, or taking a glass-bottom boat tour. The park is also home to hiking trails, kayak rentals, and picnic areas.

2. Florida Keys National Marine Sanctuary:

The Florida Keys National Marine Sanctuary is a 2,900 square mile protected area that includes coral reefs, seagrass beds, and mangrove islands. The sanctuary is home to over 6,000 species of marine life and is a popular spot for snorkeling, diving, and fishing. Visitors can explore the sanctuary by taking a boat tour or renting a kayak. The sanctuary is also home to several shipwrecks, which provide a unique opportunity for divers to explore underwater history.

3. Christ of the Abyss:

Christ of the Abyss is a statue of Jesus Christ located in the John Pennekamp Coral Reef State Park. The statue is submerged in the water and is a popular spot for divers to visit. It was placed in the park in 1965 as a tribute to Italian divers who lost their lives while diving in the area.

4. Dagny Johnson Key Largo Hammock Botanical State Park:

Dagny Johnson Key Largo Hammock Botanical State Park is a 2,400-acre park located on the northern end of the island. The park is home to several hiking trails that wind through a tropical forest of mangroves, hardwood trees, and wildflowers. The park is also home to several rare and endangered species of plants and animals, making it a popular spot for birdwatching and nature photography.

5. Key Largo Fisheries Backyard:

The Key Largo Fisheries Backyard is a popular spot for seafood lovers. This local fish market serves fresh seafood caught by local fishermen. Visitors can enjoy a casual meal in the outdoor seating area or purchase fresh fish to cook at home. The restaurant is also known for its famous Key Lime pie, which is a must-try for anyone visiting Key Largo.

6. African Queen Canal Cruise:

The African Queen is a classic boat that was used in the 1951 movie of the same name, starring Humphrey Bogart and Katharine Hepburn. The boat has been restored and is now available for public tours. Visitors can take a 90-minute cruise through the canals of Key Largo while learning about the history of the boat and the area.

7. Dolphin Research Center:

The Dolphin Research Center is a nonprofit organization that is dedicated to the study and conservation of dolphins and other marine mammals. Visitors can take a guided tour of the facility, watch dolphin shows, and even participate in interactive programs, such as swimming with dolphins.

8. Key Largo Hammocks State Botanical Site:

Key Largo Hammocks State Botanical Site is a 6.5-acre park located on the southern end of the island. The park is home to several hiking trails that wind through a forest of hardwood trees and mangroves. Visitors can also explore the park's butterfly garden and learn about the various plant and animal species that call the park home.

9. Harry Harris Beach and Park:

Harry Harris Beach and Park is a popular spot for beachgoers and families. The park features a white sandy beach, play-grounds, picnic areas, and a boat ramp. Visitors can also go fishing or swimming in the calm waters of the bay.

10. Islander Resort:

The Islander Resort is a popular resort located on the island's ocean side. The resort features a private beach, two swimming pools, a tiki bar, and several restaurants. Visitors can enjoy a relaxing vacation at the resort, which is also a popular spot for weddings and other events.

11. Key Largo Chocolates:

Key Largo Chocolates is a local chocolate shop that is known for its delicious handmade chocolates and other sweet treats.

Visitors can take a tour of the shop and see how the chocolates are made or participate in a chocolate-making workshop.

12. Pennekamp Coral Reef State Park Campground:

For visitors who want to spend more time in the park, the Pennekamp Coral Reef State Park Campground is a great option. The campground offers campsites for tents and RVs, as well as several amenities, including a camp store, picnic tables, and showers.

13. The Florida Keys Wild Bird Rehabilitation Center:

The Florida Keys Wild Bird Rehabilitation Center is a nonprofit organization that is dedicated to the rescue and rehabilitation of injured and orphaned birds in the Florida Keys. Visitors can take a guided tour of the facility and learn about the various species of birds that are treated there.

14. Spiegel Grove:

Spiegel Grove is a retired Navy ship that was intentionally sunk off the coast of Key Largo to create an artificial reef. The ship now rests in 130 feet of water and is a popular spot for advanced divers to explore.

In conclusion, Key Largo is a nature lover's paradise with a wide variety of attractions to suit every interest. From stunning coral reefs to nature parks, wildlife sanctuaries, and cultural landmarks, Key Largo has something to offer for everyone. Visitors to the island will not be disappointed by the abundance of activities available and the unique experiences that they can have.

Outdoor Activities

Key Largo is a popular destination for outdoor enthusiasts, offering a wide range of activities for visitors to enjoy. For first-time visitors, there are several outdoor activities that are must-tries when arriving on the island.

• Snorkeling and Diving:

One of the top outdoor activities in Key Largo is snorkeling and diving. The island is home to the John Pennekamp Coral Reef State Park, which is the first underwater park in the United States. Visitors can explore the park's stunning coral reefs and abundant marine life, including colorful fish, sea turtles, and even the occasional manatee. For those who have never snorkeled or dived before, there are plenty of tour operators on the island who offer guided tours for all skill levels.

• Kayaking and Paddleboarding:

Kayaking and paddleboarding are great ways to explore the island's calm waters and get up close and personal with the local wildlife. Visitors can rent kayaks and paddleboards from several rental shops on the island and paddle through the mangroves, spotting birds, fish, and other creatures along the way.

• Fishing:

Fishing is a popular activity in Key Largo, with several charter companies offering fishing trips for both novice and experienced anglers. Visitors can fish in the bay or out in the open waters of the Atlantic Ocean, catching a variety of species including bonefish, tarpon, and snapper.

· Biking:

Biking is a great way to explore Key Largo's scenic beauty at a leisurely pace. The island has several bike rental shops that offer a range of bikes, including mountain bikes and beach cruisers. Visitors can bike along the Overseas Highway, which offers stunning views of the ocean and mangrove forests.

· Hiking:

For visitors who prefer to stay on land, hiking is a great option. The Dagny Johnson Key Largo Hammock Botanical State Park is a popular hiking destination, with several trails that wind through the park's lush vegetation and wildlife. Visitors can spot birds, butterflies, and even the occasional crocodile along the way.

· Eco-Tours:

Eco-tours are a great way to learn about Key Largo's unique ecosystem and wildlife. Several tour operators offer guided tours that take visitors through the island's mangroves, highlighting the different plant and animal species that call the area home.

- Beaches:

Key Largo is home to several beautiful beaches, including John Pennekamp Coral Reef State Park Beach, Harry Harris Park Beach, and Calusa Beach. Visitors can spend a day soaking up the sun, swimming in the clear waters, and enjoying the scenery.

- Wildlife Sanctuaries:

Key Largo is home to several wildlife sanctuaries, including the Florida Keys Wild Bird Rehabilitation Center and the Dolphin Research Center. Visitors can learn about the local wildlife and even interact with some of the animals.

- Sunset Sailing:

Watching the sunset over the water is a breathtaking experience, and one of the best ways to do so in Key Largo is on a sunset sailing tour. Several tour operators offer guided tours that take visitors out onto the water, providing stunning views of the sunset and the surrounding scenery.

In conclusion, Key Largo is a paradise for outdoor enthusiasts, offering a wide range of activities for visitors to enjoy. From snorkeling and diving to kayaking, fishing, hiking, and eco-tours, there is something for everyone on the island. First-time visitors should take advantage of the opportunity to explore the island's natural beauty and wildlife, and participate in some of the many outdoor activities available.

Where to Eat

Key Largo is a beautiful destination in Florida that is known for its gorgeous beaches, crystal-clear waters, and delicious food. Whether you're a seafood lover, a fan of international cuisine, or looking for something more casual, Key Largo has plenty of options to satisfy your appetite. Here are some of the top places to eat in Key Largo:

• Sundowners

Sundowners is a popular waterfront restaurant that is known for its stunning sunsets and delicious food. The menu features a wide variety of seafood dishes, including crab cakes, shrimp scampi, and lobster tail. If you're not in the mood for seafood, they also offer steak, chicken, and pasta dishes. With indoor and outdoor seating available, Sundowners is a great place to enjoy a meal while taking in the beautiful views of the water.

• The Fish House

The Fish House is another great seafood restaurant that has been serving up fresh catches for over 25 years. They offer a variety of dishes including conch fritters, shrimp and grits, and blackened fish tacos. Their famous Fish House Punch is a must-try, made with rum, peach schnapps, and fruit juices. The restaurant has a casual, laid-back atmosphere that makes it a great spot for families.

- Snooks Bayside Restaurant & Grand Tiki Bar

If you're looking for a place to enjoy some live music while sipping on a cold drink, then Snooks Bayside Restaurant & Grand Tiki Bar is the place to be. The menu features a variety of seafood dishes, as well as burgers, salads, and sandwiches. Their signature dish is the "Snook Bites," which are lightly fried pieces of snapper served with a tangy dipping sauce. The tiki bar is the perfect spot to enjoy a sunset cocktail while taking in the beautiful views of the bay.

- Buzzard's Roost Restaurant & Bar

Buzzard's Roost Restaurant & Bar is a hidden gem located in the heart of Key Largo. The restaurant features indoor and outdoor seating, with a relaxed, tropical atmosphere. The menu includes a variety of seafood dishes, as well as burgers, sandwiches, and salads. Their conch chowder is a must-try, made with fresh conch, potatoes, and vegetables in a rich and creamy broth. The restaurant also offers live music on the weekends, making it a fun spot to hang out with friends.

- Mrs. Mac's Kitchen

Mrs. Mac's Kitchen is a Key Largo institution that has been

serving up comfort food for over 30 years. The menu includes classic dishes like meatloaf, chicken pot pie, and shrimp and grits. They are also known for their famous "World-Famous Key Lime Pie," which is a must-try for anyone visiting Key Largo. The restaurant has a cozy, homestyle atmosphere that makes it a great spot for families and groups.

- Pilot House Restaurant & Marina

Pilot House Restaurant & Marina is a popular spot for both locals and tourists alike. The restaurant features indoor and outdoor seating, with stunning views of the marina. The menu includes a variety of seafood dishes, as well as pasta, steak, and chicken dishes. They are known for their "Lazy Man's Lobster," which is a baked lobster tail served with drawn butter. The restaurant also has a sushi bar, making it a great spot for sushi lovers.

In conclusion, Key Largo is a foodie paradise with a variety of restaurants to suit every taste and budget. Whether you're in the mood for seafood, international cuisine, or classic comfort food, Key Largo has something for everyone. With its beautiful waterfront views, relaxed atmosphere, and delicious food, it's easy to see why Key Largo is a top destination for foodies. So, don't hesitate to explore the culinary scene and try out some of these amazing restaurants on your next trip to Key Largo. With so many great options to choose from, you're sure to have a memorable dining experience that will leave you satisfied and wanting to come back for more. Bon appétit!

Nightlife and Entertainment

When the sun sets over Key Largo, the party is just getting started. From live music to dancing, there's plenty of nightlife and entertainment options to choose from. Here are some of the top places to check out in Key Largo after dark:

- Caribbean Club

The Caribbean Club is a must-visit spot for anyone looking for a taste of Key Largo's history and nightlife. Built in the 1930s, this iconic bar and restaurant has been featured in several movies, including the classic film "Key Largo" starring Humphrey Bogart and Lauren Bacall. The bar features live music on the weekends and serves up delicious cocktails, including their famous Rum Runner. With its laid-back atmosphere and beautiful waterfront views, the Caribbean Club is the perfect place to relax and enjoy a night out.

- Sundowners

Sundowners is not only a great restaurant, but also a popular spot for nightlife and entertainment. On the weekends, they often have live music on the outdoor deck, which offers stunning views of the water. They also have a bar area where you can enjoy a cocktail or two while watching the sunset. With its beautiful setting and great music, Sundowners is a fun place to hang out with friends and enjoy a night out in Key Largo.

- Señor Frijoles

If you're in the mood for some Latin flavor, then Señor Frijoles is the place to be. This Mexican restaurant features a lively atmosphere and a bar that serves up a variety of tequilas and margaritas. On the weekends, they often have live music and dancing, making it a fun spot to let loose and have some fun. With its vibrant colors and festive vibe, Señor Frijoles is a great place to get a taste of Key Largo's nightlife.

- Cactus Jack's

Cactus Jack's is a popular sports bar that offers a wide variety of beers on tap and delicious pub food. They have multiple big screen TVs, making it a great spot to catch the game or watch your favorite sports team. The bar also features live music on the weekends, making it a fun place to hang out with friends and enjoy some drinks and music.

- Snooks Bayside Restaurant & Grand Tiki Bar

Snooks Bayside Restaurant & Grand Tiki Bar is not only a great restaurant, but also a popular spot for live music and dancing. On the weekends, they often have live bands playing on the outdoor stage, which offers beautiful views of the bay. They also have a large dance floor, making it a fun place to let loose and dance the night away. With its lively atmosphere and great music, Snooks Bayside Restaurant & Grand Tiki Bar is a fun place to visit in Key Largo.

- Key Largo Fisheries Backyard Cafe

Key Largo Fisheries Backyard Cafe is a hidden gem that offers a unique dining and entertainment experience. This seafood restaurant features outdoor seating in a relaxed, tropical setting. On the weekends, they often have live music playing in the background, making it a great place to unwind and enjoy some good food and drinks. They also have a dock where you can watch the boats coming in and out of the marina. With its laid-back atmosphere and great music, Key Largo Fisheries Backyard Cafe is a fun place to visit for a night out in Key Largo.

In conclusion, Key Largo offers a variety of options for nightlife and entertainment. From live music to dancing, there's something for everyone to enjoy. So, grab some friends and explore the nightlife scene in Key Largo. You're sure to have a fun and memorable night out that you won't forget.

5

Islamorada

Overview of Islamorada

Islamorada is a picturesque village located in the upper Florida Keys, nestled between the Gulf of Mexico to the west and the Atlantic Ocean to the east. The name "Islamorada" means "purple island" in Spanish and reflects the area's vibrant beauty. Known as the "Sport Fishing Capital of the World," Islamorada offers an array of outdoor activities, including fishing, diving, snorkeling, kayaking, and boating. The village consists of six small islands: Tea Table Key, Lower Matecumbe Key, Upper Matecumbe Key, Windley Key, Plantation Key, and Indian Key.

Islamorada has a rich history dating back to the early 1800s when it was a bustling trading post for ships carrying cargo between Havana and the United States. The village was also a popular spot for pirates who sought refuge in the shallow waters around the Keys. Today, visitors can learn about the area's fascinating history by visiting the Indian Key Historic State Park and the History of Diving Museum.

Fishing is the primary draw for visitors to Islamorada. The area is home to some of the world's most renowned fishing tournaments, including the Islamorada Sailfish Tournament, the World Sailfish Championship, and the Redbone Celebrity Tournament. The village has an impressive fleet of charter boats and fishing guides who can take visitors out to the deep sea to catch a variety of fish, including sailfish, marlin, tuna, and swordfish.

In addition to fishing, Islamorada offers an abundance of water activities, including kayaking, paddleboarding, snorkeling, and diving. The area's clear waters and diverse marine life make it an excellent destination for underwater exploration. Visitors can explore the shallow reefs or venture out to deeper waters to see the vibrant coral formations and exotic fish species. The nearby John Pennekamp Coral Reef State Park is a popular spot for snorkeling and diving, offering a glimpse into the diverse marine ecosystem of the Keys.

For those who prefer to stay on land, Islamorada offers plenty of opportunities for hiking, biking, and birdwatching. The area's natural beauty is on full display at the Windley Key Fossil Reef Geological State Park, which features trails through an ancient coral reef. The park is also home to numerous bird species, making it a popular spot for birdwatchers.

Islamorada is also a foodie's paradise, offering an array of dining options that range from casual beachside eateries to upscale seafood restaurants. The village is particularly renowned for its fresh seafood, including conch, lobster, and stone crab. Visitors can sample local specialties like conch fritters, lobster bisque, and key lime pie at restaurants like Islamorada Fish Company, Lazy Days Restaurant, and The Hungry Tarpon.

The village has a vibrant arts and culture scene, with numerous galleries and art studios showcasing the work of local artists. Visitors can browse through a range of artworks, from traditional paintings to contemporary sculptures, at galleries like Bluewater Potters and Gallery Morada. The Morada Way Arts & Cultural District, located in the heart of Islamorada, is home to a variety of art galleries, studios, and shops, making it a popular destination for art lovers.

Islamorada is also a popular wedding destination, thanks to its idyllic beaches, turquoise waters, and stunning sunsets. The village has numerous wedding venues, ranging from intimate beachfront ceremonies to lavish receptions in waterfront mansions. Wedding planners and vendors abound in the area, making it easy for couples to plan the perfect wedding in paradise.

Overall, Islamorada is a must-visit destination for anyone seeking a taste of paradise. Its natural beauty, rich history, and abundance of outdoor activities make it an ideal spot for adventure seekers, while its diverse dining options, arts and culture scene, and wedding venues cater to those looking for a more relaxed, indulgent vacation. Whether you're an avid fisherman, a beach lover, or a foodie, Islamorada has something for everyone. Its small-town charm, combined with its breathtaking scenery and endless recreational opportunities, make it a unique and unforgettable destination in the Florida Keys.

Top Attractions

Islamorada is a paradise for visitors looking for an escape from the hustle and bustle of city life. The village offers a wide range of attractions, from natural wonders to cultural landmarks, that are sure to keep visitors entertained throughout their stay. In this article, we will discuss the top attractions in Islamorada.

- John Pennekamp Coral Reef State Park

The John Pennekamp Coral Reef State Park is a must-visit destination for anyone interested in snorkeling or diving. Located just a short drive from Islamorada, the park features one of the most extensive coral reefs in the United States. Visitors can explore the underwater world and see colorful fish, sea turtles, and other marine life in their natural habitat.

- History of Diving Museum

The History of Diving Museum is a unique attraction that explores the history and technology of diving. The museum features a vast collection of diving equipment, including helmets, suits, and tanks, dating back to the early days of underwater exploration. Visitors can learn about the evolution of diving and see how technology has advanced over the years.

- Theater of the Sea

The Theater of the Sea is an interactive marine park that offers visitors the chance to see and interact with marine life up close. The park features a variety of shows and exhibits, including dolphin and sea lion shows, a parrot show, and a marine mammal exhibit. Visitors can also swim with dolphins, sea lions, and stingrays, making it an unforgettable experience.

· Indian Key Historic State Park

Indian Key Historic State Park is a small island located just a short boat ride from Islamorada. The island was once a thriving community, but it was destroyed by a group of Native Americans in the 1800s. Visitors can explore the ruins of the island and learn about its history through guided tours and exhibits.

· Windley Key Fossil Reef Geological State Park

The Windley Key Fossil Reef Geological State Park is a unique attraction that showcases an ancient coral reef. The park features trails that wind through the fossilized coral formations, offering visitors a glimpse into the natural history of the area. The park is also a popular spot for birdwatching, with numerous bird species living in the surrounding forests.

· Islamorada Fish Company

Islamorada Fish Company is a popular dining destination that serves fresh seafood and classic American dishes. The restaurant offers a relaxed atmosphere with stunning waterfront views, making it the perfect spot for a casual lunch or romantic dinner.

- Robbie's Marina

Robbie's Marina is a must-visit destination for anyone looking to feed the local tarpon. Visitors can purchase a bucket of fish and stand on the dock as the tarpon jump out of the water to grab a snack. The marina also offers boat rentals, fishing charters, and waterfront dining.

- Anne's Beach

Anne's Beach is a serene and picturesque beach located just south of Islamorada. The beach offers shallow waters that are perfect for swimming and relaxing. Visitors can also explore the nature trail that winds through the mangrove forests and observe the local wildlife.

- The Morada Way Arts & Cultural District

The Morada Way Arts & Cultural District is a vibrant community of art galleries, studios, and shops located in the heart of Islamorada. Visitors can browse through a range of artworks, from traditional paintings to contemporary sculptures, and attend art shows and events throughout the year.

- Florida Keys Brewing Company

The Florida Keys Brewing Company is a local brewery that offers a variety of craft beers made with local ingredients. Visitors can sample the different brews and enjoy live music and food trucks in the brewery's outdoor beer garden.

In conclusion, Islamorada is a destination that offers a range of attractions to suit any visitor's interests. From exploring the underwater world at John Pennekamp Coral Reef State Park to feeding the tarpon at Robbie's Marina, there is something for everyone in this charming village. Visitors can learn about the history of diving at the History of Diving Museum, enjoy the shows and exhibits at the Theater of the Sea, and explore the ancient coral reef at Windley Key Fossil Reef Geological State Park. For those looking for a more relaxed experience, Anne's Beach offers a picturesque and serene beach, while the Morada Way Arts & Cultural District and Florida Keys Brewing Company offer a vibrant arts and cultural scene. And of course, no visit to Islamorada is complete without indulging in the fresh seafood and stunning waterfront views at Islamorada Fish Company. Overall, Islamorada offers a unique and unforgettable experience for visitors looking to escape and enjoy the beauty and charm of the Florida Keys.

Outdoor Activities

Islamorada is a paradise for outdoor enthusiasts, offering a wide range of activities to enjoy in the beautiful natural setting of the Florida Keys. From fishing to kayaking to birdwatching, there is something for everyone to enjoy in the great outdoors in Islamorada. In this article, we will discuss some of the top outdoor activities to experience in Islamorada.

- Fishing

Fishing is one of the most popular outdoor activities in Islamorada, known as the "Sportfishing Capital of the World." The village offers a variety of fishing charters and guides, from flats fishing to deep-sea fishing. Visitors can catch a range of fish species, including bonefish, tarpon, sailfish, and tuna, among others.

- Kayaking

Kayaking is a great way to explore the natural beauty of Islamorada. Visitors can rent kayaks and explore the mangrove-lined channels and shallow waters of the backcountry. Kayaking offers a peaceful and intimate way to observe the local wildlife, including manatees, dolphins, and a variety of bird species.

- Snorkeling and Diving

Islamorada is home to one of the most extensive coral reefs in the United States, making it an excellent destination for snorkeling and diving. Visitors can explore the underwater world and see colorful fish, sea turtles, and other marine life in their natural habitat.

· Stand-Up Paddleboarding

Stand-up paddleboarding, or SUP, is a fun and easy way to explore the calm waters of Islamorada. Visitors can rent SUP boards and glide through the shallow waters, observing the local wildlife and taking in the stunning views.

· Birdwatching

Islamorada is home to a variety of bird species, making it a popular destination for birdwatchers. Visitors can observe a range of birds, including ospreys, pelicans, herons, and egrets, among others. The Windley Key Fossil Reef Geological State Park and Anne's Beach are popular spots for birdwatching.

· Biking

Biking is a great way to explore the village and take in the beautiful scenery of Islamorada. Visitors can rent bikes and ride along the Overseas Highway or explore the quiet back roads of the village. Biking offers a fun and active way to explore the area.

· Beach Activities

Islamorada is home to several stunning beaches that offer a range of activities for visitors to enjoy. Anne's Beach and Long Key State Park offer shallow waters that are perfect for swimming and relaxing. Visitors can also enjoy a variety of water sports, including kayaking, paddleboarding, and windsurfing.

· Eco-Tours

Eco-tours offer visitors a unique and educational way to explore the natural beauty of Islamorada. Visitors can take guided tours of the backcountry, observing the local wildlife and learning about the area's ecology and history.

· Sunset Cruises

Sunset cruises offer visitors a romantic and relaxing way to take in the stunning views of Islamorada. Visitors can enjoy a scenic cruise along the waters, taking in the sunset and enjoying cocktails and hors d'oeuvres.

· Golfing

Islamorada is home to several golf courses that offer stunning views and challenging courses. Visitors can enjoy a round of golf while taking in the beautiful natural scenery of the area.

In conclusion, Islamorada offers a wide range of outdoor activities for visitors to enjoy. From fishing to kayaking to birdwatching, there is something for everyone to experience in the great outdoors of this charming village. Whether you're looking for a peaceful and intimate experience or an active and adventurous one, Islamorada has something to offer.

Where to Eat

With its location, Islamorada offers a variety of dining options that cater to seafood lovers, international cuisine enthusiasts, and those seeking a casual beachfront dining experience. Here, we will explore some of the best places to eat in Islamorada.

- Lazy Days Restaurant is a must-visit destination for seafood lovers. Located on the oceanfront at 79867 Overseas Highway, Islamorada, FL 33036, this restaurant serves a variety of fresh seafood dishes that are prepared to perfection. Their menu features popular seafood dishes such as grilled octopus, yellowtail snapper, and lobster. Besides seafood, they offer other non-seafood dishes such as burgers and steak. Lazy Days has a casual atmosphere and is an ideal spot for lunch or dinner.

- Chef Michael's

Chef Michael's is a fine-dining restaurant that features an exquisite menu that incorporates fresh, locally sourced ingredients. The menu changes frequently to feature the seasonal ingredients, but some favorites include the seared duck breast, pork chop, and the seafood risotto. Chef Michael's also features an extensive wine list that pairs perfectly with the dishes. You'll find them at 81671 Overseas Highway, Islamorada, FL 33036.

- Morada Bay Beach Cafe

Morada Bay Beach Cafe is a popular beachfront dining spot that is perfect for enjoying the beautiful sunset while savoring delicious dishes. The cafe serves a variety of seafood dishes such as conch fritters, grilled Mahi-Mahi, and lobster mac and cheese. They also serve other non-seafood dishes such as tacos, sandwiches, and salads. With its location on the beach, Morada Bay Beach Cafe provides a casual and relaxing dining experience. You'll find them at 81600 Overseas Highway, Islamorada, FL 33036.

- Midway Cafe & Coffee Bar

For those seeking a quick bite to eat or a morning coffee, Midway Cafe & Coffee Bar is the perfect spot. This cozy cafe serves a variety of breakfast sandwiches, wraps, and bagels. They also serve coffee and tea beverages, smoothies, and juices. The cafe has a laid-back atmosphere, making it an ideal spot to relax and enjoy a morning coffee while taking in the beautiful scenery. You can reach them at 80499 Overseas Highway, Islamorada, FL 33036.

- Island Grill

The Island Grill is a casual dining spot that serves a variety of seafood and non-seafood dishes. Their menu features dishes such as fish tacos, shrimp scampi, and buffalo chicken sandwiches. The Island Grill also has a lively atmosphere, with live music and a tiki bar. It is a perfect spot for a fun evening out. You'll find them at 85501 Overseas Highway, Islamorada, FL 33036.

· Green Turtle Inn

The Green Turtle Inn is a historic landmark in Islamorada and has been a dining destination for more than 70 years. The restaurant serves a variety of dishes that incorporate fresh, locally sourced ingredients. The menu features popular dishes such as the shrimp and grits, grilled yellowtail snapper, and the lobster thermidor. The Green Turtle Inn has a warm and inviting atmosphere, making it an ideal spot for a romantic evening out. They are located at 81219 Overseas Highway, Islamorada, FL 33036.

In conclusion, Islamorada offers a variety of dining options that cater to different tastes and preferences. From fine-dining to casual beachfront dining, visitors can enjoy fresh seafood, international cuisine, and other non-seafood dishes. Whether you're seeking a romantic evening out or a fun evening with friends, the restaurants in Islamorada will cater to your needs.

Nightlife and Entertainment

While Islamorada may be best known for its beautiful beaches, water activities, and delicious cuisine, the nightlife and entertainment scene in this Florida Keys destination is definitely worth exploring. Whether you're looking for a relaxing night out or an exciting evening filled with music and dancing, Islamorada offers a variety of entertainment options to cater to your preferences. Here are some of the best places to experience nightlife and entertainment in Islamorada.

• The Lorelei Cabana Bar and Restaurant

Located on the bayside of Islamorada, The Lorelei Cabana Bar and Restaurant is a popular spot for both locals and tourists alike. The cabana bar offers stunning sunset views and live music on most evenings, creating a lively atmosphere perfect for a night out. The restaurant features a seafood-focused menu, with dishes such as fish tacos, lobster bisque, and seared tuna. The Lorelei is also known for its famous frozen drinks, including the Painkiller and the Rum Runner, which are perfect for sipping on a warm summer evening.

• Smuggler's Cove

If you're looking for a lively atmosphere with a bit of a pirate twist, Smuggler's Cove is the place for you. This tiki bar offers nightly entertainment, including live music and karaoke, as well as themed events and parties throughout the year. Smuggler's Cove has an extensive drink menu, featuring tropical cocktails, frozen drinks, and a variety of beers and wines. The bar also offers a small food menu, with dishes such as fish dip, conch fritters, and shrimp tacos.

• The Green Turtle Inn

The Green Turtle Inn, which we mentioned earlier as a top restaurant in Islamorada, also offers a lively nightlife scene. The bar at The Green Turtle Inn offers a variety of craft cocktails, wines, and beers, as well as a small bites menu featuring dishes such as oysters, deviled eggs, and a cheese board. The bar hosts regular events, including live music and trivia nights, making it a great spot for a fun night out with friends.

- The Morada Bay Beach Cafe

The Morada Bay Beach Cafe, another popular restaurant we mentioned earlier, offers a unique evening experience with its Full Moon Parties. These parties take place once a month, typically around the full moon, and feature live music, dancing, and fire performances on the beach. The Morada Bay Beach Cafe also hosts other special events throughout the year, including wine dinners and holiday celebrations.

- The Trading Post

The Trading Post is a unique shopping and dining destination in Islamorada that also offers a bit of evening entertainment. The Trading Post features a courtyard area where live music is performed on most evenings, creating a fun and lively atmosphere. The venue also offers a variety of craft cocktails, beer, and wine, as well as a food menu featuring dishes such as tacos, burgers, and sandwiches.

· Theater of the Sea

For a family-friendly evening activity, consider visiting Theater of the Sea. This marine park offers evening programs that allow visitors to experience the park's marine life in a unique way. The evening programs include a sunset dolphin encounter, a sea lion show, and a night snorkel adventure. These programs offer a unique way to experience the marine life of the Florida Keys while also providing a fun evening activity for the whole family.

In conclusion, while Islamorada may not be known for its nightlife and entertainment scene as much as some other destinations, this Florida Keys destination offers a variety of options for those seeking an exciting evening out. From lively beachfront bars to unique events and experiences, visitors to Islamorada are sure to find something to suit their preferences.

6

Marathon

Overview of Marathon

Located in the heart of the Florida Keys, Marathon is a popular destination for travelers seeking a tropical paradise filled with sun, sand, and sea. With its warm climate, crystal-clear waters, and abundance of outdoor activities, Marathon offers visitors the ultimate vacation experience.

Geography and Climate:

Marathon is situated in the middle of the Florida Keys, about halfway between Key West and Miami. The city spans 10 islands, including Boot Key, Grassy Key, and Vaca Key, and is connected by the Overseas Highway, which stretches 113 miles from Key Largo to Key West. The climate in Marathon is tropical, with temperatures averaging in the mid to high 80s Fahrenheit (around 30 degrees Celsius) during the summer months and mid to high 70s Fahrenheit (around 25 degrees Celsius) during the winter months. The area is also prone to occasional tropical storms and hurricanes, particularly during the Atlantic hurricane season from June to November.

Activities:

Marathon is a haven for outdoor enthusiasts, with a wide range of activities available for visitors to enjoy. The city's location in the Florida Keys makes it the perfect place to experience all kinds of water activities, such as swimming, snorkeling, scuba diving, kayaking, paddleboarding, and fishing. The area's coral reefs are some of the most vibrant and diverse in the world, making it a popular destination for snorkelers and divers.

For those who prefer to stay on land, Marathon offers plenty of opportunities for hiking, biking, and wildlife watching. The city is home to several parks and nature reserves, including the Marathon Wild Bird Center and the Crane Point Hammock Museum and Nature Center, where visitors can explore the local flora and fauna.

Accommodations:

Marathon offers a wide range of accommodations to suit every budget and preference. From luxurious resorts and hotels to quaint bed and breakfasts and vacation rentals, visitors to Marathon can find a place to stay that fits their needs. Many of the city's accommodations are situated along the water, offering breathtaking views of the ocean and easy access to water activities.

Dining:

Marathon is known for its delicious cuisine, particularly its seafood. With its location on the water, the city offers an abundance of fresh seafood options, from conch fritters and lobster bisque to grilled mahi-mahi and blackened snapper. The area is also home to several popular seafood restaurants, including The Island Fish Co., Castaway Waterfront Restaurant and Sushi Bar, and The Keys Fisheries Market and Marina.

Culture and History:

Marathon has a rich cultural and historical heritage, with a variety of attractions and landmarks that showcase the area's unique past. The city is home to the Marathon Community Theatre, which hosts regular performances and events, as well as several art galleries and museums. The Pigeon Key Foundation and Marine Science Center offers visitors a chance to learn about the history of the area's bridges and the marine life of the Florida Keys.

Another important landmark in Marathon is the Seven Mile Bridge, which spans the ocean between Marathon and Little Duck Key. The bridge was originally built in the early 1900s as part of the Florida East Coast Railway and has since been rebuilt and renovated several times. Today, it serves as a popular spot for sightseeing and fishing.

Events:

Marathon is home to several annual events and festivals that attract visitors from around the world. One of the most popular events is the Marathon Seafood Festival, which takes place every March and features live music, local seafood vendors, and family-friendly activities. The city also hosts the Marathon Games, a multi-sport event that includes activities such as kayaking, swimming, and running.

Conclusion:

Marathon is a tropical paradise that offers visitors a wide range of activities and experiences. With its crystal-clear waters,

abundance of outdoor activities, and rich cultural and historical heritage, Marathon is the perfect destination for anyone seeking a vacation that combines relaxation, adventure, and learning. Whether you're a water sports enthusiast, a nature lover, or a history buff, Marathon has something to offer everyone.

One of the things that sets Marathon apart from other destinations is its location in the middle of the Florida Keys. This makes it the perfect base from which to explore the surrounding area, whether you want to visit nearby islands or take a day trip to Key West. The Overseas Highway, which connects Marathon to the rest of the Keys, is itself a scenic route that offers breathtaking views of the ocean and the surrounding landscape.

Another thing that makes Marathon unique is its focus on conservation and sustainability. The city is home to several parks and nature reserves that are dedicated to protecting the local environment, and many of its restaurants and accommodations prioritize sustainable practices and locally sourced ingredients.

Overall, Marathon is a vibrant and welcoming community that offers visitors the chance to experience the best of the Florida Keys. Whether you're looking for a romantic getaway, a family vacation, or an outdoor adventure, Marathon is the perfect destination for you.

Top Attractions

Marathon offers visitors a wide range of attractions and activities to enjoy. Whether you're a nature lover, a history buff, or an adventure seeker, there's something for everyone in Marathon. Here are some of the top attractions in Marathon:

1.Sombrero Beach: One of the most popular attractions in Marathon is Sombrero Beach, a stunning white-sand beach that stretches for miles along the Atlantic Ocean. With crystal-clear waters, soft sand, and plenty of amenities, including picnic tables, showers, and a playground, Sombrero Beach is the perfect place to spend a day soaking up the sun and enjoying the ocean.

2. Dolphin Research Center: The Dolphin Research Center is a must-visit attraction for animal lovers. This nonprofit organization is dedicated to the study and care of dolphins and other marine mammals and offers visitors the chance to interact with these intelligent and playful creatures. Visitors can swim with dolphins, feed them, and even paint with them.

3. The Turtle Hospital: The Turtle Hospital is another popular attraction in Marathon that is dedicated to the rehabilitation and conservation of sea turtles. Visitors can take a guided tour of the facility and learn about the hospital's efforts to rescue, rehabilitate, and release injured sea turtles back into the wild. The hospital also has a gift shop where visitors can purchase souvenirs and support the organization's conservation efforts.

4. Curry Hammock State Park: Curry Hammock State Park is a 1,000-acre park located on Little Crawl Key and is a popular

destination for outdoor enthusiasts. The park features a pristine beach, hiking trails, and campsites for overnight stays. Visitors can enjoy swimming, kayaking, fishing, and birdwatching in this beautiful natural setting.

5. The Crane Point Museum and Nature Center: The Crane Point Museum and Nature Center is a 63-acre nature preserve and museum that offers visitors a glimpse into the rich history and ecology of the Florida Keys. The center features exhibits on the area's native plants and animals, as well as artifacts and exhibits on the area's history and culture. Visitors can also take a guided tour of the historic Adderley House, a restored 1903 Florida Keys home.

6. Seven Mile Bridge: The Seven Mile Bridge is one of the most iconic landmarks in the Florida Keys and is a must-visit attraction for anyone traveling to Marathon. The bridge was originally built in the early 1900s as part of the Florida East Coast Railway and now serves as a popular spot for fishing, sightseeing, and enjoying breathtaking views of the ocean and the surrounding islands.

7. Pigeon Key Foundation and Marine Science Center: The Pigeon Key Foundation and Marine Science Center is a nonprofit organization dedicated to preserving the history of the Florida Keys and educating visitors about the marine environment. The center offers guided tours of the island of Pigeon Key, which served as a base for workers building the Overseas Highway in the early 1900s. Visitors can also learn about the marine life of the Florida Keys and participate in hands-on educational activities.

8. Marathon Wild Bird Center: The Marathon Wild Bird Center is a rehabilitation center for injured and orphaned birds and is dedicated to the conservation and protection of the area's native bird species. Visitors can take a guided tour of the facility and learn about the center's efforts to care for and release injured birds back into the wild.

9. Grassy Keys Aquarium Encounters: Grassy Keys Aquarium Encounters is a unique attraction that offers visitors the chance to get up close and personal with a variety of marine animals. Visitors can snorkel with sharks, feed stingrays, and interact with other marine creatures in this immersive and educational environment.

10. Captain Hook's Marina and Dive Center: Captain Hook's Marina and Dive Center is the perfect destination for scuba diving enthusiasts. The center offers a range of diving trips and courses, including wreck dives, reef dives, and night dives. Visitors can also rent equipment and book snorkeling trips to explore the beautiful waters surrounding Marathon.

11. Florida Keys Aquarium Encounters: Florida Keys Aquarium Encounters is another popular attraction in Marathon that offers visitors the chance to get up close and personal with marine life. Visitors can feed sharks and rays, snorkel in a coral reef exhibit, and explore the center's exhibits on marine biology and conservation.

12. Marathon Community Park: Marathon Community Park is a 33-acre park that offers a wide range of recreational activities for visitors of all ages. The park features a playground, sports

fields, a fitness trail, and a skate park, as well as picnic areas and pavilions for family gatherings and events.

13. Island Hopper Boat Rentals: Island Hopper Boat Rentals offers visitors the chance to explore the Florida Keys by boat. Visitors can rent a variety of boats, from small skiffs to large pontoons, and explore the area's beautiful waterways, including the Gulf of Mexico and the Atlantic Ocean.

14. Historic Pigeon Key: Historic Pigeon Key is a small island located just off the coast of Marathon that played an important role in the construction of the Overseas Highway. Visitors can take a ferry to the island and explore its historic buildings and exhibits, including the old railroad museum and the Pigeon Key Foundation.

15. Marathon Theater: The Marathon Theater is a local landmark that has been entertaining visitors for over 70 years. The theater features a variety of live performances, including plays, musicals, and concerts, as well as classic films and documentaries.

Overall, Marathon offers visitors a wealth of attractions and activities to enjoy, from beautiful beaches and nature reserves to historic landmarks and cultural institutions. Whether you're looking for a relaxing getaway or an adventure-packed vacation, Marathon is the perfect destination for you.

Outdoor Activities

Marathon is a paradise for outdoor enthusiasts. With its beautiful beaches, clear blue waters, and lush natural landscapes,

Marathon offers a wealth of outdoor activities for visitors to enjoy.

1.Snorkeling and Scuba Diving: Marathon is home to some of the most spectacular coral reefs in the world, making it an ideal destination for snorkeling and scuba diving. Visitors can explore the coral reefs and encounter a wide variety of marine life, including tropical fish, sea turtles, and even sharks. Popular dive sites include Sombrero Reef, Coffin's Patch, and Looe Key Reef.

2. Fishing: Marathon is also known as the "Sport Fishing Capital of the World," thanks to its rich abundance of game fish. Visitors can charter a boat and head out to the open waters to try their luck at catching a variety of fish, including sailfish, marlin, tuna, and wahoo.

3. Kayaking and Paddleboarding: With its calm, clear waters, Marathon is a great destination for kayaking and paddleboarding. Visitors can rent a kayak or paddleboard and explore the area's many waterways, including the Gulf of Mexico and the Atlantic Ocean. Popular spots include the mangrove-lined canals of Boot Key Harbor and the crystal-clear waters of Curry Hammock State Park.

4. Beaches: Marathon boasts several beautiful beaches, including Sombrero Beach, Coco Plum Beach, and Curry Hammock State Park. These beaches offer visitors the perfect place to relax, swim, and soak up the sun. Visitors can also enjoy a variety of water activities, such as snorkeling, paddleboarding, and kayaking.

5. Biking and Hiking: Marathon offers several biking and hiking trails for visitors to explore. The Florida Keys Overseas Heritage Trail is a popular trail that runs through Marathon and offers stunning views of the water and surrounding landscapes. Visitors can also explore the trails at Curry Hammock State Park, which wind through mangrove forests and offer great views of the Gulf of Mexico.

6. Wildlife Viewing: Marathon is home to a wide variety of wildlife, including manatees, sea turtles, and a variety of bird species. Visitors can take a wildlife tour and explore the area's natural habitats, including the mangrove forests and seagrass beds. Visitors can also take a trip to the Crane Point Nature Center, which offers exhibits on the area's natural history and wildlife.

7. Golfing: Marathon boasts several world-class golf courses, including the Sombrero Country Club and the Florida Keys Country Club. These courses offer stunning views of the water and surrounding landscapes, as well as challenging holes for golfers of all skill levels.

8. Eco Tours: Visitors can take an eco-tour and explore the area's natural habitats and wildlife. These tours offer visitors the chance to learn about the area's unique ecosystem and the efforts to conserve it. Visitors can take a tour of the Dolphin Research Center or the Turtle Hospital and learn about these amazing creatures and their conservation.

9. Sunset Cruises: Marathon offers stunning sunset views over the water, and visitors can take a sunset cruise to experience

the beauty of the area. These cruises offer visitors the chance to relax and enjoy the views while sipping on cocktails and enjoying live music.

In conclusion, Marathon offers a wealth of outdoor activities for visitors to enjoy. From snorkeling and fishing to kayaking and hiking, there's something for everyone in Marathon. Whether you're a thrill-seeker or just looking for a relaxing getaway, Marathon is the perfect destination for outdoor adventure.

Where to Eat

Marathon offers a diverse culinary scene with a variety of dining options to satisfy any craving. Here are some of the top places to eat in Marathon:

1.Keys Fisheries Market & Marina: This waterfront restaurant and seafood market is a must-visit for seafood lovers. Known for their famous lobster Reuben sandwich, this family-owned and operated restaurant also offers a variety of fresh seafood dishes, including grilled fish, fried shrimp, and conch fritters. Visitors can also watch the boats come in and unload their catches at the marina.

2. The Island Fish Co.: Another waterfront restaurant, The Island Fish Co. offers stunning views of the water and a menu that features fresh seafood, sushi, and tropical cocktails. The restaurant's outdoor tiki bar and live music make it a popular spot for happy hour and sunset views.

3. Butterfly Cafe: Located at the Tranquility Bay Beachfront Resort, the Butterfly Cafe is a hidden gem that offers upscale

dining in a relaxed, beachfront setting. The menu features fresh, locally-sourced seafood, steak, and vegetarian options, and the restaurant's outdoor patio offers stunning views of the water.

4. Barracuda Grill: This cozy, family-owned restaurant offers a menu that combines Caribbean and Mediterranean flavors with locally-sourced seafood and produce. The restaurant's outdoor seating area is surrounded by lush vegetation, creating a tranquil dining experience.

5. Frank's Grill: This no-frills diner-style restaurant is a popular spot for breakfast and lunch, with a menu that includes classic American dishes like pancakes, omelets, and burgers. The restaurant's outdoor patio offers a casual, laid-back atmosphere.

6. Castaway Waterfront Restaurant & Sushi Bar: Located on the water, Castaway offers a menu that features fresh seafood, sushi, and tropical cocktails. The restaurant's outdoor seating area and live music make it a popular spot for happy hour and sunset views.

7. Lighthouse Grill: Located at the Faro Blanco Resort & Yacht Club, the Lighthouse Grill offers a menu that features locally-sourced seafood and steak, as well as an extensive wine list. The restaurant's outdoor seating area offers stunning views of the water and the Seven Mile Bridge.

8. Brutus Seafood Market & Eatery: This casual seafood restaurant and market offers a variety of fresh seafood dishes, including crab cakes, conch fritters, and fried shrimp. The market also

sells fresh seafood to take home and cook yourself.

9. Marathon Grill and Ale House: This casual restaurant and bar offers a menu that features classic American pub food, including burgers, wings, and sandwiches. The restaurant's outdoor seating area and live music make it a popular spot for happy hour and late-night dining.

10. Sweet Savannah's: This bakery and cafe offers a menu that features homemade pastries, breakfast sandwiches, and coffee. Visitors can enjoy their breakfast or lunch on the outdoor patio, surrounded by lush vegetation.

In conclusion, Marathon offers a diverse culinary scene with a variety of dining options to satisfy any craving. From waterfront seafood restaurants to cozy cafes, there's something for everyone in Marathon. Whether you're looking for a casual, laid-back dining experience or an upscale, romantic dinner, Marathon has it all.

Nightlife and Entertainment

While Marathon may be known for its stunning beaches and outdoor activities, the city also offers a variety of nightlife and entertainment options for visitors and locals alike. From live music and dancing to late-night bars and lounges, there's something for everyone to enjoy. Here are some of the top nightlife and entertainment options in Marathon:

1.Sunset Grille & Raw Bar: This waterfront restaurant and bar is known for its live music and daily sunset celebrations. The restaurant's outdoor seating area offers stunning views of the water, and the bar features a variety of tropical cocktails and local craft beers.

2. Sparky's Landing: This waterfront restaurant and bar is a popular spot for live music and dancing. The restaurant's outdoor patio features live bands and DJs, and the bar offers a variety of drinks, including frozen cocktails and local craft beers.

3. Overseas Lounge: This casual lounge is a popular spot for locals, offering a variety of drinks and a laid-back atmosphere. The bar features live music on the weekends, and visitors can enjoy their drinks on the outdoor patio.

4. The Hurricane: This lively bar and restaurant offers a variety of drinks and a menu that features classic pub food, including burgers, wings, and sandwiches. The bar's outdoor seating area is a popular spot for happy hour and late-night drinks.

5. Castaway Waterfront Restaurant & Sushi Bar: While known for its seafood and sushi, Castaway also offers live music and entertainment on the weekends. The restaurant's outdoor seating area and waterfront location make it a popular spot for happy hour and sunset views.

6. Boondocks Grille & Draft House: This sports bar and restaurant features a variety of drinks and a menu that includes classic pub food and seafood dishes. The restaurant's outdoor seating area offers views of the water and a relaxed, laid-back atmosphere.

7. Marathon Community Theatre: This local theater offers a variety of live performances, including plays, musicals, and concerts. The theater's intimate setting allows for an up-close and personal experience with the performers.

8. Sunset Cinema: This outdoor movie theater offers free movies on the beach during the summer months. Visitors can bring their own chairs or blankets and enjoy a movie under the stars.

9. Crane Point Museum & Nature Center: While not specifically a nightlife or entertainment venue, Crane Point offers a variety of events and activities throughout the year, including concerts and educational programs. Visitors can also enjoy the center's walking trails and wildlife exhibits.

10. Sombrero Country Club: This local country club offers a variety of events and activities throughout the year, including live music and dancing. The club's outdoor seating area and golf course views make it a popular spot for happy hour and late-night drinks.

In conclusion, while Marathon may be a laid-back beach town, it still offers a variety of nightlife and entertainment options for visitors and locals. Whether you're looking for live music and dancing, a casual bar atmosphere, or outdoor movie screenings, there's something for everyone to enjoy in Marathon. So, after a long day of outdoor activities, be sure to check out one of these top nightlife and entertainment venues and experience the vibrant and lively side of Marathon.

7

Big Pine Key and the Lower Keys

Overview of Big Pine Key and the Lower Keys

Big Pine Key and the Lower Keys are a cluster of islands located in the southernmost part of the Florida Keys. This area is known for its pristine waters, stunning coral reefs, and abundant wildlife, making it a popular destination for nature enthusiasts, scuba divers, and anglers.

Big Pine Key is the largest of the Lower Keys and is located about 30 miles east of Key West. The island is home to the National Key Deer Refuge, which was established in 1957 to protect the endangered Key deer. These miniature deer are a unique feature of the island and can often be seen grazing along the roadsides.

The Lower Keys, including Big Pine Key, are also known for their excellent fishing opportunities. The surrounding waters are home to a variety of game fish, including tarpon, bonefish, permit, and snook. Anglers can fish from shore, wade in the shallow flats, or book a charter boat for a guided fishing experience.

The Lower Keys also offer plenty of opportunities for snorkeling and diving. Looe Key Reef, located just offshore from Big Pine Key, is a popular dive site known for its colorful coral formations and diverse marine life, including sea turtles, rays, and schools of tropical fish.

In addition to its natural beauty, Big Pine Key and the Lower Keys offer a laid-back, relaxed atmosphere that is perfect for those looking to escape the hustle and bustle of city life. Visitors can spend their days lounging on the beach, kayaking through mangrove forests, or exploring the many art galleries and boutiques that dot the islands.

One of the main attractions of the Lower Keys is the Seven Mile Bridge, a historic bridge that connects the islands of Marathon and Little Duck Key. The bridge offers stunning views of the surrounding waters and is a popular spot for fishing and sightseeing.

For those looking for a more adventurous experience, the Lower Keys offer plenty of opportunities for kayaking, paddleboarding, and camping. Bahia Honda State Park, located on the island of the same name, is a popular destination for camping and outdoor recreation. The park features beautiful beaches, hiking trails, and campsites that are just steps away from the water.

Overall, Big Pine Key and the Lower Keys offer a unique blend of natural beauty and laid-back charm that is sure to appeal to anyone looking for a relaxing vacation. Whether you are interested in fishing, diving, or just lounging on the beach, this area has something for everyone.

Top Attractions

Big Pine Key and the Lower Keys are a treasure trove of natural beauty and unique attractions that draw visitors from all over the world. From stunning beaches to fascinating wildlife, here are some of the top attractions to check out when visiting this beautiful area.

- National Key Deer Refuge

The National Key Deer Refuge is a must-see attraction for nature lovers. Established in 1957 to protect the endangered Key deer, this refuge covers over 8,500 acres of land on Big Pine Key and several surrounding islands. Visitors can take a guided tour to learn more about the refuge and its inhabitants, or explore on their own via hiking or biking trails.

- Looe Key Reef

Looe Key Reef, located just offshore from Big Pine Key, is a world-renowned dive site that is home to an abundance of marine life. The reef is known for its colorful coral formations and diverse ecosystem, which includes sea turtles, stingrays, and schools of tropical fish. Visitors can take a guided dive tour, or simply snorkel and explore the reef on their own.

- Bahia Honda State Park

Bahia Honda State Park is a pristine beach and natural preserve that is located on the island of the same name. The park features crystal-clear waters, white sand beaches, and a variety of outdoor activities such as fishing, kayaking, and camping. There are also several hiking trails that offer stunning views of the surrounding landscape.

· Dolphin Research Center

The Dolphin Research Center is a nonprofit organization that is dedicated to the study and conservation of dolphins and other marine mammals. Visitors can take guided tours to learn about the center's research and rehabilitation efforts, or participate in a swim or interaction program with the dolphins themselves.

· Seven Mile Bridge

The Seven Mile Bridge is a historic bridge that connects the islands of Marathon and Little Duck Key. The bridge is a popular spot for fishing and sightseeing, and offers stunning views of the surrounding waters. Visitors can also take a sunset or sunrise stroll along the bridge for a truly unforgettable experience.

· Curry Hammock State Park

Curry Hammock State Park is a 1,200-acre park located on Little Crawl Key. The park features a variety of outdoor activities, including kayaking, fishing, and camping. Visitors can also explore the park's natural beauty on hiking and biking trails, or relax on the pristine beaches.

· Big Pine Kayak Adventures

Big Pine Kayak Adventures offers guided tours and rentals for kayaking and paddleboarding throughout the Lower Keys. Visitors can explore the mangrove forests and shallow flats that surround the islands, and learn about the local ecology and wildlife.

· Old Wooden Bridge Fishing Camp

The Old Wooden Bridge Fishing Camp is a unique campground and marina that is located on Big Pine Key. Visitors can rent RV or tent camping sites, or stay in one of the camp's rustic cabins. The camp also offers a variety of fishing charters and excursions, as well as kayak and paddleboard rentals.

· No Name Key

No Name Key is a small island located just off the coast of Big Pine Key. The island is home to a community of residents who have chosen to live off the grid, relying on solar and wind power for their electricity. Visitors can take a guided tour of the island to learn more about sustainable living and the unique community that calls it home.

· Key West Butterfly and Nature Conservatory

While technically located in Key West, the Key West Butterfly and Nature Conservatory is a must-see attraction for anyone visiting the Lower Keys. This indoor conservatory is home to over 50 species of butterflies, as well as a variety of exotic birds and plants. Visitors can take a guided tour or simply wander through the tranquil, tropical setting.

Outdoor Activities

Big Pine Key and the Lower Keys are a great place for outdoor activities, with plenty of opportunities to enjoy the beautiful natural surroundings. Here are some outdoor activities that visitors can enjoy in this area:

1.Snorkeling and Diving: The crystal clear waters surrounding Big Pine Key and the Lower Keys are perfect for snorkeling and diving. The area is home to the only living coral reef system in the continental United States, and there are plenty of dive sites to explore. Looe Key Reef, located about 5 miles south of Big Pine Key, is a popular spot for both snorkelers and divers.

2. Fishing: The waters surrounding Big Pine Key and the Lower Keys are home to a variety of fish, including tarpon, bonefish, and permit. Visitors can hire a charter boat and spend the day fishing, or simply cast a line from one of the many bridges that span the area's channels and canals.

3. Kayaking and Paddleboarding: The calm, shallow waters surrounding Big Pine Key and the Lower Keys are perfect for kayaking and paddleboarding. Visitors can rent a kayak or

paddleboard and explore the area's mangrove-lined waterways, or simply paddle along the coastline and take in the beautiful views.

4. Hiking and Nature Trails: The Florida Keys are home to a variety of unique plant and animal species, and visitors can explore the area's natural beauty by hiking one of the many nature trails. The National Key Deer Refuge on Big Pine Key has several hiking trails that offer visitors the chance to see the endangered Key deer, as well as a variety of bird species and other wildlife.

5. Beaches: The Lower Keys are home to some of the most beautiful beaches in the Florida Keys. Bahia Honda State Park, located on Big Pine Key, has a beautiful beach with clear turquoise waters and white sand. Visitors can swim, sunbathe, and even camp at the park.

6. Wildlife Viewing: Big Pine Key and the Lower Keys are home to a variety of unique wildlife species, including the endangered Key deer, which can be seen throughout the area. Visitors can also spot a variety of bird species, including the white-crowned pigeon, the roseate spoonbill, and the osprey.

7. Camping: For visitors who want to spend the night in the great outdoors, there are several camping options in Big Pine Key and the Lower Keys. Bahia Honda State Park offers both tent and RV camping, and there are several private campgrounds in the area as well.

Overall, Big Pine Key and the Lower Keys offer visitors a variety of outdoor activities to enjoy. From snorkeling and diving to hiking and wildlife viewing, there is something for everyone in this beautiful part of the Florida Keys.

Where to Eat

When it comes to dining in Big Pine Key and the Lower Keys, visitors will find a variety of options ranging from casual seafood shacks to fine dining establishments. Here are some of the top places to eat in the area:

1.Square Grouper Bar and Grill:

Located in Cudjoe Key, Square Grouper Bar and Grill is a waterfront restaurant that offers beautiful views of the ocean. The restaurant serves up a variety of seafood dishes, including conch fritters, fried shrimp, and grilled mahi-mahi. The restaurant also has a full bar, and live music is often featured on the weekends.

2. Boondocks Grille and Draft House:

Located in Ramrod Key, Boondocks Grille and Draft House is a family-friendly restaurant that offers indoor and outdoor seating. The restaurant serves up a variety of dishes, including seafood, burgers, and salads. The restaurant also has a mini-golf course and an arcade, making it a great place to bring the kids.

3. Mangrove Mama's: Located on Sugarloaf Key, Mangrove Mama's is a funky, tropical-themed restaurant that serves Caribbean-inspired dishes. The menu features dishes such as jerk chicken, conch chowder, and seafood gumbo. The restaurant also has a large outdoor seating area and a tiki bar.

Overall, whether visitors are looking for casual seafood shacks or fine dining experiences, Big Pine Key and the Lower Keys offer a range of delicious options to choose from. With so many great restaurants to choose from, visitors are sure to find something to satisfy their appetites during their time in the area.

8

Key West

Overview of Key West

Key West is a small island located at the southernmost point of the United States, just 90 miles from Cuba. With its tropical climate, crystal-clear waters, and vibrant cultural scene, it has become a popular destination for travelers seeking a laid-back, beachy getaway.

History and Culture

Key West has a rich history that is reflected in its architecture, museums, and cultural institutions. The island was first inhabited by indigenous tribes before being claimed by the Spanish in the 16th century. It later became an important port for pirates and then a hub for the cigar-making industry.

In the late 1800s, Key West became home to a thriving literary community, with writers like Ernest Hemingway and Tennessee Williams spending time on the island. Today, visitors can explore many of the historic homes and buildings that once housed these famous writers, as well as museums dedicated to their legacies.

Attractions

Key West is home to a variety of attractions that offer something for everyone. Some of the most popular include:

Duval Street: This iconic street is home to many of Key West's best bars, restaurants, and shops. It's a great place to stroll, people-watch, and take in the island's lively atmosphere.

Ernest Hemingway Home and Museum: This beautiful home was once the residence of the famous writer Ernest Hemingway. Today, visitors can tour the home and learn about Hemingway's life and work, as well as meet the descendants of his beloved six-toed cats.

Mallory Square: This waterfront square is famous for its nightly sunset celebration, where visitors gather to watch the sun set over the water and enjoy street performers and vendors.

Key West Butterfly and Nature Conservatory: This indoor attraction allows visitors to walk through a tropical paradise filled with exotic butterflies and birds.

Key West Aquarium: Visitors can get up close and personal with a variety of sea creatures, including sharks, sea turtles, and stingrays.

Outdoor Activities

Key West's beautiful natural surroundings offer plenty of

opportunities for outdoor activities. Some of the most popular include:

Snorkeling and Diving: Key West's coral reefs are home to a diverse array of marine life, making it a popular destination for snorkeling and diving enthusiasts.

Fishing: With its clear waters and abundance of fish, Key West is a great place for fishing. Visitors can take a charter boat out for a day of deep-sea fishing, or try their luck from shore.

Beaches: Key West has several beautiful beaches, including Smathers Beach, Higgs Beach, and Fort Zachary Taylor State Park. Visitors can swim, sunbathe, and enjoy a variety of water sports.

Biking: Key West is a small island that is easy to explore by bike. Visitors can rent a bike and pedal their way around the island, taking in the sights and sounds of this tropical paradise.

Nightlife and Entertainment

Key West's nightlife scene is legendary, with plenty of options for those looking to party into the night. Some of the most popular bars and clubs include:

1.Sloppy Joe's Bar: This iconic bar was a favorite of Ernest Hemingway and is still a popular spot for live music and cold drinks.

2. The Green Parrot Bar: Another Key West institution, the Green Parrot is known for its lively atmosphere and live music.

3. Irish Kevin's: This bar is known for its raucous, interactive entertainment, including live music, comedy, and karaoke.

4. Rick's Bar: This multi-level bar and nightclub offers a variety of music and entertainment options, including DJs, live bands, and comedy shows.

Food and Drink

Key West is a foodie's paradise, with a variety of restaurants and eateries that showcase the island's fresh seafood and tropical flavors

Some of the must-try restaurants in Key West include:

1.Blue Heaven: This popular restaurant is known for its Caribbean-inspired cuisine, including dishes like jerk chicken and conch fritters. Visitors can dine al fresco in the restaurant's beautiful courtyard, which is filled with tropical plants and roaming chickens.

2. Louie's Backyard: This elegant restaurant offers stunning ocean views and a menu of fresh seafood and international flavors. Visitors can dine on the restaurant's outdoor terrace or in the chic indoor dining room.

3. Santiago's Bodega: This tapas restaurant is a local favorite, offering a variety of small plates that showcase flavors from around the world. Visitors can enjoy their meal in the cozy indoor dining room or in the restaurant's charming outdoor courtyard.

4. Hogfish Bar and Grill: This casual restaurant is located on the waterfront and is known for its fresh seafood and laid-back atmosphere. Visitors can dine outside on the restaurant's covered patio or inside in the cozy dining room.

5. Kermit's Key West Key Lime Shoppe: No trip to Key West is complete without trying the island's signature dessert: key lime pie. Kermit's is known for its delicious pies, as well as a variety of other key lime-flavored treats, including cookies and ice cream.

In addition to its great restaurants, Key West also has a thriving bar scene. Visitors can enjoy a tropical cocktail at one of the island's many beachfront bars or dive into a local watering hole for a cold beer and some live music.

Overall, Key West is a vibrant and exciting destination that offers something for everyone. Whether visitors are looking to soak up the sun on the beach, explore the island's rich history and culture, or party into the night, they are sure to find what they're looking for in this tropical paradise.

IV

Part Four

9

Day Trips and Excursions from the Florida Keys

The Florida Keys offer a wealth of opportunities for day trips and excursions, allowing visitors to explore the surrounding area and discover all the natural beauty and cultural attractions of the region. From snorkeling and diving trips to visits to nearby state parks and historical landmarks, there is no shortage of activities to choose from.

One of the most popular day trips from the Florida Keys is to visit the nearby Dry Tortugas National Park, located about 70 miles west of Key West. This remote island park is only accessible by boat or seaplane, and features stunning coral reefs, crystal-clear waters, and a historic Civil War-era fort that visitors can explore.

Another popular excursion is to take a snorkeling or diving trip to the nearby Looe Key National Marine Sanctuary, located just off the coast of Big Pine Key. This protected reef system is home to a variety of marine life, including colorful fish, sea turtles, and even the occasional shark.

For those interested in history and culture, a visit to the nearby city of Miami is a must. Just a few hours' drive from the Florida Keys, Miami offers a vibrant arts and cultural scene, as well as world-famous beaches and iconic landmarks like the art deco district and the Freedom Tower.

Other popular day trips and excursions from the Florida Keys include visits to nearby state parks like Bahia Honda State Park and John Pennekamp Coral Reef State Park, as well as guided tours of the Everglades National Park or the Florida Keys National Wildlife Refuge.

Whether visitors are looking for outdoor adventure, cultural exploration, or just a relaxing day spent soaking up the sun, there are plenty of day trips and excursions to choose from in and around the Florida Keys.

Dry Tortugas National Park
Dry Tortugas National Park is a remote island paradise located about 70 miles west of Key West. The park is only accessible by boat or seaplane, making it a perfect destination for a day trip or excursion. Visitors to the park can explore the pristine beaches, crystal-clear waters, and historic fort, as well as enjoy a variety of outdoor activities like snorkeling, fishing, and birdwatching.

One popular day trip from the Dry Tortugas National Park is to visit nearby Fort Jefferson National Monument. This massive fortress was built in the 1800s and served as a military prison during the Civil War. Today, visitors can tour the fort and learn about its history, as well as enjoy the stunning views of the surrounding waters and nearby islands.

Another popular day trip from the Dry Tortugas is to go snorkeling or diving in the nearby coral reefs. The reefs surrounding the park are home to a variety of marine life, including colorful fish, sea turtles, and even the occasional shark. Visitors can book a guided snorkeling or diving tour from Key West or take a private boat out to explore the reefs on their own.

For those looking for a more relaxed day trip, a visit to one of the nearby uninhabited islands is a must. The nearby Marquesas Keys and Loggerhead Key offer stunning beaches, clear waters, and plenty of opportunities for beachcombing and exploring.

Finally, visitors to the Dry Tortugas National Park can also take a seaplane or boat ride to nearby Key West for a day of shopping, dining, and sightseeing. Key West is known for its lively arts and culture scene, as well as its world-famous beaches and historic landmarks.

Whether visitors are looking for outdoor adventure, historical exploration, or just a relaxing day spent soaking up the sun, there are plenty of day trips and excursions to choose from when visiting the Dry Tortugas National Park. With its stunning natural beauty and rich history, this remote island paradise is a must-visit destination for anyone traveling to the Florida Keys.

Everglades National Park

Everglades National Park is one of the most unique and fascinating ecosystems in the world, and visitors to the park can explore its vast wetlands, dense mangrove forests, and abundant wildlife. While there is plenty to see and do within the park itself, there are also many day trips and excursions available that allow visitors to explore the surrounding area.

One popular day trip from Everglades National Park is to take an airboat tour of the nearby swamps and wetlands. These tours offer a unique way to experience the beauty and diversity of the Everglades, as visitors glide across the water and spot alligators, birds, and other wildlife.

Another popular day trip is to visit the nearby Big Cypress National Preserve. This massive park encompasses over 700,000 acres of swamps, wetlands, and forests, and is home to a variety of wildlife, including the elusive Florida panther. Visitors can hike, bike, or take a guided tour to explore the park's many trails and waterways.

For those interested in history and culture, a visit to nearby Homestead, Florida is a must. This small town is home to a variety of historic sites and museums, including the Coral Castle Museum and the Fruit & Spice Park, which showcases the region's unique agricultural history.

Other popular day trips and excursions from Everglades National Park include visits to nearby state parks like Collier-Seminole State Park and Fakahatchee Strand Preserve State Park, as well as guided tours of the Ten Thousand Islands and the Gulf of Mexico.

Whether visitors are looking for outdoor adventure, cultural exploration, or just a relaxing day spent soaking up the sun, there are plenty of day trips and excursions to choose from in and around Everglades National Park. With its stunning natural beauty and rich history, this unique ecosystem is a must-visit destination for anyone traveling to the Florida Keys.

Miami and South Florida

A day trip to Miami and South Florida can offer visitors a taste of the vibrant culture, beautiful beaches, and exciting nightlife that this region is famous for. While a day may not be enough to see and do everything, there are still plenty of opportunities to explore and experience the best that Miami and South Florida have to offer.

One popular destination for a day trip to Miami is South Beach, located on the southern tip of Miami Beach. This iconic neighborhood is known for its stunning art deco architecture, white sandy beaches, and lively nightlife. Visitors can stroll along the famous Ocean Drive, visit the Versace Mansion, and take in the sights and sounds of this colorful and eclectic neighborhood.

Another must-see destination in Miami is Little Havana, the city's Cuban cultural center. Visitors can experience the sights, sounds, and flavors of this vibrant neighborhood by visiting local shops and cafes, taking a walking tour, or attending a live music or dance performance.

For those interested in history and art, a visit to the Vizcaya Museum and Gardens is a must. This stunning estate, located just a short drive from Miami, features a beautiful Italian Renaissance-style villa and over 10 acres of lush gardens and

97

grounds.

Of course, these are just a few of the many destinations and activities available for visitors to Miami and South Florida. From world-class dining and shopping to exciting outdoor adventures and cultural experiences, there is something for everyone in this vibrant and diverse region.

Overall, a day trip to Miami and South Florida can be a great way to experience the best of this dynamic and exciting destination. Whether visitors are interested in history, art, culture, or just soaking up the sun on one of the region's many beautiful beaches, there is no shortage of things to see and do in this vibrant and diverse region.

10

Practical Information and Extras

Safety and Health

When planning a trip to the Florida Keys, it's important to prioritize your safety and health. The beautiful beaches, warm waters, and lively nightlife can be enjoyable, but they also pose potential hazards. To ensure a safe and healthy trip, here are some practical tips for first-time visitors to the Florida Keys.

· Sun Safety

The Florida Keys have a tropical climate, which means hot and humid weather conditions all year round. While this makes it perfect for outdoor activities, it also means you need to take extra care to avoid sunburn and heat exhaustion. Wear a wide-brimmed hat, sunglasses, and sunscreen with a high SPF to protect your skin. Remember to reapply every two hours, especially after swimming or sweating. Stay hydrated by drinking plenty of water throughout the day.

- Water Safety

The Florida Keys offer a wide range of water activities such as snorkeling, diving, and kayaking. While these activities are enjoyable, they also pose potential hazards. Always wear a lifejacket when on a boat or participating in water activities. Be aware of your surroundings, tides, and weather conditions, and never swim alone. Avoid touching or feeding marine animals, as they can be dangerous and harmful.

- Mosquito and Bug Protection

The Florida Keys are home to many mosquitoes and other bugs, particularly during the warmer months. Protect yourself by wearing long-sleeved shirts and pants, using insect repellent, and staying indoors during dawn and dusk when mosquitoes are most active. To avoid attracting bugs, avoid wearing perfumes or scented lotions.

- Food and Water Safety

The Florida Keys have a variety of restaurants and food options to choose from. However, it's important to prioritize food and water safety to avoid food poisoning or waterborne illnesses. Stick to bottled water and avoid drinking tap water. Only eat food that is thoroughly cooked and served hot. Wash your hands frequently, especially before eating.

- Driving Safety

If you plan on renting a car, be aware of the unique driving conditions in the Florida Keys. The Overseas Highway, the main road connecting the islands, can be narrow and winding in some areas. Be cautious of other drivers, especially during peak tourist season. Observe speed limits and traffic signals, and always wear your seatbelt.

- Emergency Preparedness

In case of an emergency, it's important to be prepared. Familiarize yourself with the location of the nearest hospital or urgent care center. Keep important documents such as your passport, ID, and travel insurance in a safe place. If you plan on participating in water activities, consider wearing a waterproof pouch to keep your phone and other valuables safe.

- COVID-19 Precautions

As with any travel destination, it's important to follow the current COVID-19 guidelines and precautions. The Florida Keys require face masks in indoor public areas and encourage social distancing. Check for updates on the Florida Keys tourism website and the Centers for Disease Control and Prevention (CDC) website before your trip.

In conclusion, prioritizing your safety and health is crucial when visiting the Florida Keys. Be aware of the potential hazards and take necessary precautions to ensure a safe and enjoyable trip. By following these tips, you can have a memorable experience in this tropical paradise.

Money and Currency

When planning a trip to the Florida Keys, it's important to understand the money and currency system to avoid any financial issues during your visit. Here are some practical tips for first-time visitors to the Florida Keys regarding money and currency.

· Currency

The currency used in the United States, including the Florida Keys, is the US dollar. Bills come in denominations of $1, $5, $10, $20, $50, and $100. Coins come in denominations of 1 cent (penny), 5 cents (nickel), 10 cents (dime), 25 cents (quarter), and 50 cents (half dollar). It's a good idea to have a mix of bills and coins with you for small purchases and tipping.

· Payment Methods

In the Florida Keys, most businesses accept credit and debit cards, including Visa, MasterCard, American Express, and Discover. However, some smaller businesses may only accept cash, so it's always a good idea to have some on hand. Some businesses may also accept mobile payment methods such as Apple Pay or Google Wallet. It's always a good idea to check with the business ahead of time to see which payment methods they accept.

· Tipping

Tipping is a common practice in the United States, including the Florida Keys. It's customary to tip 15-20% of the total bill at restaurants, bars, and for services such as haircuts or massages. It's also common to tip hotel staff such as bellhops and housekeepers. When in doubt, ask locals or check for tipping guidelines posted in the establishment.

· ATM and Banks

ATMs are widely available throughout the Florida Keys, particularly in larger towns such as Key West and Marathon. Most ATMs will charge a transaction fee, so it's a good idea to withdraw larger amounts of cash at once to avoid multiple fees. Banks are also available throughout the Florida Keys, including Bank of America, Chase, and Wells Fargo. It's always a good idea to inform your bank of your travel plans to avoid any issues with your account.

· Exchange Rates

If you are traveling from outside the United States, it's important to understand the exchange rate between your currency and the US dollar. The exchange rate can fluctuate daily, so it's a good idea to check with your bank or a currency exchange service ahead of time. It's also important to note that many businesses may not accept foreign currency, so it's a good idea to exchange your currency for US dollars before your trip.

· Sales Tax

Sales tax is added to most purchases in the Florida Keys, including restaurants, bars, and shopping. The sales tax rate in Monroe County, which includes the Florida Keys, is 7.5%. This tax is added to the total bill, so be prepared to pay a little extra on top of the listed prices.

· Budgeting

The cost of living and traveling in the Florida Keys can vary depending on the time of year and your activities. It's a good idea to create a budget before your trip to avoid overspending. Research activities and attractions ahead of time to get an idea of prices, and consider using a travel rewards credit card to earn points or miles for future trips.

In conclusion, understanding the money and currency system in the Florida Keys is important for a smooth and enjoyable trip. Be prepared with a mix of cash and cards, and don't forget to tip appropriately. With these tips in mind, you can enjoy your trip without any financial worries.

Shopping

Florida Keys is a beautiful vacation destination, and shopping is one of the exciting activities to do during your trip. Here are some practical tips for shopping in Florida Keys:

1.Visit local markets: Florida Keys has many local markets that sell unique and handmade items, such as paintings, crafts, and jewelry. Visiting these markets is a great way to support local businesses and get unique souvenirs.

2. Check the hours of operation: Before planning your shopping trip, make sure to check the hours of operation of the stores you want to visit. Some stores may close early or have different opening hours on weekends and holidays.

3. Bring cash: While most stores in Florida Keys accept credit cards, some may only accept cash. It's a good idea to bring some cash with you when shopping to avoid any inconvenience.

4. Be prepared for the weather: Florida Keys can get quite hot and humid, especially during the summer months. Make sure to wear light clothing, comfortable shoes, and carry a hat and sunscreen to protect yourself from the sun.

5. Look out for sales: Many stores in Florida Keys offer discounts and sales throughout the year. Keep an eye out for signs and flyers advertising these sales to get the best deals.

6. Ask for recommendations: If you're not sure where to shop, ask the locals for recommendations. They will be happy to suggest their favorite stores and markets.

7. Buy local products: Florida Keys is known for its fresh seafood,

Key lime pie, and conch fritters. Make sure to try these local delicacies and buy them from local shops and markets to support the local economy.

8. Negotiate prices: While negotiating prices is not common in most stores, it's worth trying in some markets and shops. If you're buying multiple items or spending a significant amount of money, you may be able to negotiate a better price.

9. Keep an eye on your belongings: Florida Keys is a popular tourist destination, and theft can be a problem in some areas. Keep your belongings close to you and be cautious when shopping in crowded areas.

10. Have fun: Shopping in Florida Keys can be a fun and memorable experience. Don't stress too much about finding the perfect souvenirs and enjoy the unique atmosphere and beautiful surroundings.

In conclusion, shopping in Florida Keys is a great way to support local businesses, find unique souvenirs, and enjoy the beautiful surroundings. With these practical tips, you can make the most out of your shopping experience and have a memorable vacation.

Local Markets and Boutiques

The Florida Keys are a chain of islands located off the southern coast of Florida. They are known for their beautiful beaches, stunning coral reefs, and tropical weather. In addition to these natural attractions, the Florida Keys are home to a wide variety of local markets and boutiques that offer unique shopping experiences for visitors.

One of the most popular local markets in the Florida Keys is the Key West Farmers Market. This market is held every Thursday from 10 am to 2 pm at Bayview Park in Key West. Visitors can browse through a variety of vendors selling fresh produce, artisanal bread, honey, spices, and more. In addition to food, the market also features handmade crafts, jewelry, and clothing from local artisans. The Key West Farmers Market is a great place to find unique souvenirs and gifts to take home.

Another popular local market in the Florida Keys is the Islamorada Art Walk. This event is held on the third Thursday of every month from 6 pm to 9 pm in the Morada Way Arts and Cultural District in Islamorada. The Art Walk features over a dozen local artists and artisans showcasing their work, including paintings, sculptures, jewelry, and other handmade goods. Visitors can also enjoy live music, food vendors, and drinks from local breweries and distilleries.

For those looking for unique and high-end boutique shopping, the Florida Keys offer a variety of options. In Key West, visitors can find a number of high-end boutiques along Duval Street. These stores offer everything from designer clothing and accessories to home decor and art. Some notable boutiques include Kate Spade, Lilly Pulitzer, and Michael Kors.

In Marathon, visitors can explore the many boutiques and galleries located in the Art District. Here, visitors can find locally-made art, jewelry, and home decor items. Some popular stores include the Rain Barrel Artisan Village, which features over 30 artists selling their work, and the Blue Bamboo Gallery, which specializes in contemporary art and photography.

Another popular boutique shopping destination in the Florida Keys is the Village of Islamorada. Here, visitors can find a variety of unique stores selling clothing, accessories, and gifts. Some popular boutiques include the Island Bazaar, which offers a wide variety of beachwear and souvenirs, and the Purple Isles Artisans, which features a collection of locally-made crafts and jewelry.

For those looking for a more authentic local shopping experience, the Florida Keys also offer a number of flea markets and thrift stores. One of the most popular flea markets is the Big Pine Flea Market, located in Big Pine Key. This market features over 100 vendors selling everything from antiques and collectibles to fresh produce and baked goods.

In addition to the Big Pine Flea Market, visitors can also explore a number of thrift stores and consignment shops throughout the Florida Keys. These stores offer a variety of unique and affordable items, including clothing, accessories, home decor, and more. Some popular thrift stores include the Community Thrift Store in Marathon and the Guilded Peach in Key West.

Overall, the Florida Keys offer a wide variety of local markets and boutiques for visitors to explore. Whether you're looking for high-end designer boutiques or authentic flea markets, there is something for everyone in the Florida Keys. So next time you're planning a trip to this tropical paradise, be sure to set aside some time for a little shopping!

Souvenirs From Florida Keys

The Florida Keys are a unique and vibrant destination that attracts visitors from all over the world. Whether you are looking for beautiful beaches, stunning coral reefs, or vibrant culture and history, the Florida Keys have something for everyone. When it comes to souvenirs, there are plenty of options for visitors to choose from. Here are some popular souvenirs that visitors can get from the Florida Keys.

- Key Lime Products

One of the most popular souvenirs from the Florida Keys is anything related to key lime. Key lime is a small, tart lime that is grown in the Florida Keys and used in many local dishes, including the famous key lime pie. Visitors can find a wide variety of key lime products, including key lime pie mix, key lime jelly, key lime cookies, and key lime candies. These products make for great gifts or a sweet treat to take home and enjoy.

- Nautical Items

The Florida Keys are surrounded by beautiful waters, making nautical items a popular souvenir choice. Visitors can find a variety of nautical items, such as seashell crafts, sailboat models, and anchors. Local artists also create unique nautical-themed artwork, including paintings, sculptures, and photography.

- Conch Shell Products

Conch shells are a staple of the Florida Keys, and visitors can find a wide variety of conch shell products, including jewelry, ornaments, and figurines. The conch shell is a symbol of the Florida Keys and is often used in local art and decor. Visitors can also purchase actual conch shells to take home as a unique souvenir.

- T-Shirts and Apparel

T-shirts and apparel are a classic souvenir option for visitors to the Florida Keys. Many local stores offer a wide variety of designs, featuring everything from local landmarks and wildlife to quirky slogans and sayings. Visitors can also find a variety of hats, sunglasses, and other accessories to complete their Florida Keys look.

- Artwork and Photography

The Florida Keys are home to a thriving art community, and visitors can find a wide variety of unique artwork and photography to take home as a souvenir. Local artists create pieces inspired by the natural beauty and vibrant culture of the Florida Keys, including paintings, sculptures, and photography. Visitors can also find prints and postcards featuring iconic Florida Keys landmarks and scenery.

- Spices and Seasonings

The Florida Keys are known for their unique cuisine, and visitors can take home a taste of the Keys with them through spices and seasonings. Local shops offer a wide variety of seasonings, including seafood rubs, jerk seasoning, and key lime pepper. These spices make for great gifts and can add a little taste of the Florida Keys to any home-cooked meal.

· Seashells

Seashells are a popular souvenir choice for visitors to the Florida Keys. The islands are home to a wide variety of seashells, including conch shells, starfish, and sand dollars. Visitors can find seashells for sale at local shops, or they can take a stroll on the beach and collect their own.

In conclusion, the Florida Keys offer a wide variety of souvenirs for visitors to take home and enjoy. From key lime products and nautical items to artwork and seashells, there is something for everyone. These souvenirs are not only a great way to remember your trip to the Florida Keys but also support local businesses and artisans. So next time you visit this tropical paradise, be sure to bring a little piece of the Florida Keys home with you.

Local Customs and Etiquette

Florida Keys is a unique region with a rich cultural heritage and a laid-back lifestyle. As a tourist, it is essential to understand the local customs and etiquette to make the most out of your visit. Here are some tips to keep in mind when exploring the Florida Keys:

· Dress Code

Florida Keys has a relaxed dress code, but it is advisable to dress appropriately for the activity and the weather. Lightweight and comfortable clothes, such as shorts and t-shirts, are ideal for exploring the beaches and enjoying the sun. However, if you are planning to visit upscale restaurants or bars, it is advisable to dress up a bit.

· Greetings

When meeting someone for the first time in the Florida Keys, a friendly smile and a handshake will suffice. People in the Florida Keys are generally friendly and welcoming, and it is common to exchange pleasantries with strangers. It is also common to use "ma'am" and "sir" as a sign of respect when addressing someone.

· Punctuality

In the Florida Keys, the pace of life is slower than in other regions of the United States. However, it is still considered rude to be late for a meeting or an appointment. If you are running late, it is polite to inform the other person in advance.

· Tipping

Tipping is a common practice in the Florida Keys, and it is

customary to tip 15-20% of the total bill at restaurants, bars, and for services such as haircuts or massages. It is also common to tip hotel staff such as bellhops and housekeepers.

· Beach Etiquette

The beaches in the Florida Keys are public, and it is essential to respect other visitors. It is customary to leave the beach cleaner than you found it, and to dispose of any trash in designated bins. It is also essential to be respectful of other visitors' space and not to play loud music or engage in disruptive behavior.

· Driving

Driving is a common way to get around the Florida Keys, and it is important to follow the local traffic rules. Speed limits are strictly enforced, and it is illegal to drink and drive. It is also essential to yield to pedestrians and cyclists, as they have the right of way in designated areas.

· Environmental Awareness

Florida Keys is home to a diverse ecosystem, including coral reefs and mangroves. It is essential to be aware of your impact on the environment and to take steps to minimize your carbon footprint. This includes using environmentally friendly products and reducing waste.

· Respect Local Traditions

The Florida Keys has a rich cultural heritage, and it is essential to respect local traditions and customs. This includes respecting the rights of indigenous peoples and not engaging in cultural appropriation. It is also important to respect local religious customs and practices.

In conclusion, understanding the local customs and etiquette in the Florida Keys is crucial to having a positive and enjoyable experience. By being respectful of the local culture and environment, you can make the most of your visit and leave a positive impression on the locals.

Packing List

Packing for a trip to the Florida Keys can be a bit tricky, as the weather can be quite variable depending on the time of year. Additionally, the Keys are known for their laid-back and casual atmosphere, so your wardrobe should reflect that. Here is a general packing list to help you prepare for your trip:

1.Clothing

As previously mentioned, the Florida Keys have a very casual atmosphere, so lightweight and comfortable clothing is a must. It's also important to remember that the Keys are located in a tropical climate, so be sure to pack clothing that will keep you cool and comfortable in the heat. Some suggested items include:

· T-shirts and tank tops
· Shorts

- Light dresses or skirts
- Bathing suits and cover-ups
- Flip flops or sandals
- Comfortable walking shoes
- Light sweater or jacket for cooler evenings
- Sun Protection

2. The Florida Keys are known for their beautiful beaches and abundant sunshine, but that also means it's important to take steps to protect your skin. Be sure to pack:

- Sunscreen with a high SPF (at least 30)
- Sunglasses
- Wide-brimmed hat
- Insect Repellent

3. The Florida Keys are also known for their mosquitoes and other biting insects, especially during the summer months. Be sure to pack insect repellent to keep bugs at bay.

4. Water Activities Gear

The Florida Keys are famous for their water activities such as snorkeling, diving, and fishing. Be sure to pack any gear you may need for these activities, such as:

- Snorkel and mask
- Swim fins

- Dive certification card
- Fishing gear (if you plan to fish)
- Electronics

5. If you plan to take photos or stay connected while on your trip, be sure to pack:

- Camera or smartphone with a good camera
- Chargers and cables
- Power bank (to recharge your electronics on the go)

6. Other Essentials
Don't forget these important items as well:

- Personal toiletries (toothbrush, toothpaste, shampoo, etc.)
- Medications (if you take any)
- First aid kit (including items such as band-aids and pain relievers)
- Cash and credit cards (many businesses in the Keys may not accept all credit cards)
- Beach bag or backpack to carry your essentials
- Light rain jacket (in case of rain)

While this is a basic packing list, it's important to consider the time of year you are visiting as well. During the winter months, the Keys can experience cooler temperatures, so be sure to pack a light jacket or sweater. In the summer, be sure to pack plenty of lightweight and breathable clothing, as well as sun protection.

It's also important to note that many activities in the Keys involve being on the water, so it's a good idea to pack clothes that can get wet. Additionally, some restaurants and other establishments may have dress codes, so it's a good idea to bring at least one nicer outfit in case you decide to go out to a fancy dinner or event.

Finally, be sure to pack everything in a suitcase or backpack that is easy to carry and maneuver. The Keys are made up of several islands connected by bridges, so you may need to transport your luggage from one location to another.

In conclusion, packing for a trip to the Florida Keys should be relatively easy, as the casual atmosphere and tropical climate allow for comfortable and lightweight clothing. Be sure to pack items for sun protection, water activities, and insect repellent, as well as any other essentials you may need. By packing smart, you can make the most of your trip and enjoy all that the Florida Keys have to offer.

Useful Websites and Apps

As a first-time visitor to the Florida Keys, there are many websites and apps that can help make your trip smoother and more enjoyable. Here are some of the most useful ones:

· Visit Florida Keys

The Visit Florida Keys website is a great resource for planning your trip. It has information on everything from accommodations and dining to events and activities. You can also request a free travel guide and sign up for a monthly e-newsletter to stay up-to-date on the latest news and events.

· Key West Express

Key West Express is a ferry service that provides transportation from Fort Myers and Marco Island to Key West. Their website is a great resource for checking schedules and booking tickets. The ferry ride is a great way to see the beautiful scenery of the Florida Keys and avoid traffic on the highway.

· Waze

Waze is a navigation app that can help you avoid traffic and get to your destination quickly. It uses real-time traffic data to suggest the fastest routes and can provide turn-by-turn directions.

· The Weather Channel

The Weather Channel app is a great resource for checking the weather in the Florida Keys. It can provide hourly and daily forecasts, as well as alerts for severe weather.

· Yelp

Yelp is a popular app for finding restaurants and other businesses in the area. It has reviews and ratings from other users, as well as menus and photos. It can be a great tool for finding hidden gems and local favorites.

• Airbnb

Airbnb is a popular platform for booking vacation rentals. It can be a great option for staying in the Florida Keys, as it allows you to stay in a local neighborhood and have access to amenities such as a kitchen and laundry facilities.

• AllTrails

AllTrails is a hiking and outdoor activity app that provides trail maps, reviews, and photos. It can be a great resource for finding hiking trails and outdoor activities in the Florida Keys.

• Uber/Lyft

Uber and Lyft are ride-sharing apps that can be a convenient and cost-effective way to get around the Florida Keys, especially if you don't want to rent a car.

Florida Keys National Marine Sanctuary

The Florida Keys National Marine Sanctuary website is a great resource for learning about the area's marine life and conservation efforts. It has information on snorkeling and diving locations, as well as rules and regulations for protecting the environment.

· TripIt

TripIt is a travel organization app that can help keep all of your travel plans in one place. It can store your flight information, hotel reservations, and other travel details, as well as provide alerts for flight delays and changes.

In conclusion, these websites and apps can help first-time visitors to the Florida Keys plan their trip, navigate the area, and find the best activities and amenities. With these resources, you can make the most of your trip and have a memorable experience in the beautiful Florida Keys.

11

Final Thoughts on the Florida Keys

I n conclusion, the Florida Keys is a truly unique and stunning destination that offers something for everyone. Whether you're an outdoor enthusiast, a foodie, or just looking to relax on a beautiful beach, the Keys has it all. By following the tips above, you can ensure that your Florida Keys vacation is a success. So, start planning your trip now, and get ready to create unforgettable memories that will last a lifetime. From the stunning sunsets to the clear blue waters, the Florida Keys is a destination that you won't want to miss in 2023. So, pack your bags, and get ready for an adventure that you'll never forget!

Happy Travels!

Printed in Great Britain
by Amazon

25626458R00076